QUOTATIONS

for

SPEECHES

QUOTATIONS

for

SPEECHES

BLOOMSBURY

First edition published 1992

This edition published 2000

Copyright © Bloomsbury Publishing Plc 1992, 2000

Bloomsbury Publishing Plc, 38 Soho Square, London W1V 5DF

Extracts from the Authorized King James Version of the Bible, which is Crown Copyright, are reproduced by permission of Eyre and Spottiswoode, Her Majesty's Printers.

British Library Cataloguing in Publication Data

A CIP catalogue record for this book is available from the British Library

ISBN 0 7475 5040 9

Compiled and typeset by
Market House Books, Ltd., Aylesbury
Printed and bound in Great Britain by
Clays Ltd, St Ives Plc

Acknowledgments

Editor

John Daintith

Contributors

Fran Alexander
Peter Blair
Elizabeth Bonham
Alan Isaacs
Jonathan Law
Sandra McQueen
Elizabeth Martin
Jessica Scholes
Gwen Shaw
Anne Stibbs
Brenda Tomkins
Linda Wells
Edmund Wright

CONTENTS

INTRODUCTION

This book is a collection of over 1000 quotations designed to be used by anyone who wants to make or write a speech. The quotations have been chosen for their aptness or wit or their relevance to a particular topic.

The first part of the book has a short section of quotations about speeches and speech making. Then follows the main body of the quotations, arranged under a series of topic headings. These headings appear in alphabetical order. A list of the topics is given overleaf. Under each topic heading, the quotations are numbered and arranged in alphabetical order by the author's name.

Two indexes appear at the end of the book to help the user. The first is based on the *keyword* or *-words* in a quotation. This index will be of use to anyone who can remember part of a quotation and wishes to locate it and check its source. The second index is a name index, useful for those seeking appropriate quotations by their favourite writers or speakers. Both indexes direct the reader to the topic under which the quotation appears and to its number.

Of course, people who make or write speeches should use their own words; it is, however, sometimes useful to have help. As Anatole France said, 'When a thing has been said and said well, have no scruple. Take it and copy it.'

We hope that this book will be useful to people who have no scruples about saying things well.

The Editor

LIST OF TOPICS

SPEECHES

INTRODUCTIONS

Ways to start a speech?

1 If there are any of you at the back who do not hear me, please don't raise your hands because I am also nearsighted.

W. H. Auden (1907–73)
British poet.
Starting a lecture in a large hall

2 I want to reassure you I am not this size, really – dear me no, I'm being amplified by the mike.

G. K. Chesterton (1874–1936)
British writer.
At a lecture in Pittsburgh

3 Wery glad to see you indeed, and hope our acquaintance may be a long 'un, as the gen'l'm'n said to the fi' pun' note.

Charles Dickens (1812–70)
British novelist.

4 I think it's the most extraordinary collection of talent, of human knowledge, that has ever been gathered together at the White House – with the possible exception of when Thomas Jefferson dined alone.

John Fitzgerald Kennedy (1917–63)
US statesman.
Said at a dinner for Nobel Prizewinners, 29 Apr 1962

5 I want to thank you for stopping the applause. It is impossible for me to look humble for any period of time.

Henry Kissinger (1923–)
German-born US politician and diplomat.

6   I declare this thing open – whatever it is.

Prince Philip (1921–)
The consort of Queen Elizabeth II.
Opening a new annex at Vancouver City Hall

QUOTATIONS ABOUT SPEECHES
How (or how not) to do it

7   Begin low, speak slow; take fire, rise higher; when most impressed be self-possessed; at the end wax warm, and sit down in a storm.

Anonymous

8   This is a rotten argument, but it should be good enough for their lordships on a hot summer afternoon.

Anonymous
A note on a ministerial brief read out by mistake in the House of Lords

9   Let thy speech be short, comprehending much in few words; be as one that knoweth and yet holdeth his tongue.

Bible: Ecclesiasticus

10   I take the view, and always have done, that if you cannot say what you have to say in twenty minutes, you should go away and write a book about it.

Lord Brabazon of Tara (1910–74)
British businessman and Conservative politician.

11   Adepts in the speaking trade
Keep a cough by them ready made.

Charles Churchill (1731–64)
British poet.

12 The art of making deep sounds from the stomach sound like important messages from the brain.

Winston Churchill (1874–1965)
British statesman.
On the art of speechmaking

13 He is one of those orators of whom it was well said, 'Before they get up they do not know what they are going to say; when they are speaking, they do not know what they are saying; and when they sit down, they do not know what they have said'.

Winston Churchill
Referring to Lord Charles Beresford

14 A good storyteller is a person who has a good memory and hopes other people haven't.

Irvin S. Cobb (1876–1944)
US writer.

15 I dreamt that I was making a speech in the House. I woke up, and by Jove I was!

Duke of Devonshire (1833–1908)
Conservative politician.

16 A good indignation makes an excellent speech.

Ralph Waldo Emerson (1803–82)
US poet and essayist.

17 Why doesn't the fellow who says, 'I'm no speechmaker', let it go at that instead of giving a demonstration.

F. McKinney Hubbard (1868–1930)
US journalist.

18 A speech is like a love affair: any fool can start one but to end it requires considerable skill.

Lord Mancroft (1917–87)
British businessman and writer.

19 What orators lack in depth they make up to you in length.

Baron de Montesquieu (1688–1755)
French writer.

20 Be sincere, be brief, be seated.

Franklin D. Roosevelt (1882–1945)
US Democratic president.

21 Brevity is the soul of wit.

William Shakespeare (1564–1616)
English dramatist.

22 For I have neither wit, nor words, nor worth,
Action, nor utterance, nor the power of speech,
To stir men's blood; I only speak right on.

William Shakespeare

23 It usually takes more than three weeks to prepare a good impromptu speech.

Mark Twain (Samuel Langhorne Clemens; 1835–1910)
US writer.

24 Don't quote Latin; say what you have to say, and then sit down.

Duke of Wellington (1769–1852)
British general and statesman.
Advice to a new Member of Parliament

THE AUDIENCE

25 If there is anyone here whom I have not insulted, I beg his pardon.

Johannes Brahms (1833–97)
German composer.

26 I always enjoy appearing before a British audience. Even if they don't feel like laughing, they nod their heads to show they've understood.

Bob Hope (Leslie Townes Hope; 1903–)
British-born US comedian.

27 I quite agree with you, sir, but what can two do against so many?

George Bernard Shaw (1856–1950)
Irish dramatist and critic.
Responding to a solitary hiss heard amongst the applause at the first performance of *Arms and the Man* in 1894

28 I would just like to mention Robert Houdin who in the eighteenth century invented the vanishing bird-cage trick and the theater matinée – may he rot and perish. Good afternoon.

Orson Welles (1915–85)
US film actor.
Addressing the audience at the end of a matinée performance

29 The play was a great success, but the audience was a disaster.

Oscar Wilde (1854–1900)
Irish-born British dramatist.
Referring to a play that had recently failed

QUOTATIONS ABOUT TOPICS

ABSTINENCE

1   He neither drank, smoked, nor rode a bicycle. Living frugally, saving his money, he died early, surrounded by greedy relatives. It was a great lesson to me.

John Barrymore (1882–1942)
US actor.

2   We might as well make up our minds that chastity is no more a virtue than malnutrition.

Alex Comfort (1920–2000)
US physician and author.

3   Teetotallers lack the sympathy and generosity of men that drink.

W. H. Davies (1871–1940)
British poet.

4   It was a brilliant affair; water flowed like champagne.

William M. Evarts (1818–1901)
US lawyer and statesman.
Describing a dinner given by US President Rutherford B. Hayes
(1877–81), an advocate of temperance

5   If you resolve to give up smoking, drinking and loving, you don't actually live longer; it just seems longer.

Clement Freud (1924–)
British Liberal politician and broadcaster.

6   Mr Mercaptan went on to preach a brilliant sermon on that melancholy sexual perversion known as continence.

Aldous Huxley (1894–1964)
British novelist.

7 Lastly (and this is, perhaps, the golden rule), no woman should marry a teetotaller, or a man who does not smoke.

Robert Louis Stevenson (1850–94)
Scottish writer.

ACHIEVEMENT

1 There is no such thing as a great talent without great will-power.

Honoré de Balzac (1799–1850)
French novelist.

2 Genius is one per cent inspiration and ninety-nine per cent perspiration.

Thomas Edison (1847–1931)
US inventor.

3 Because it is there.

George Mallory (1886–1924)
British mountaineer.
Answer to the question 'Why do you want to climb Mt. Everest?'

4 For years politicians have promised the moon, I'm the first one to be able to deliver it.

Richard Milhous Nixon (1913–94)
US president.

5 A genius! For thirty-seven years I've practiced fourteen hours a day, and now they call me a genius!

Pablo Sarasate (1844–1908)
Spanish violinist and composer.
On being hailed as a genius by a critic

6 I did not write it. God wrote it. I merely did his dictation.

Harriet Beecher Stowe (1811–96)
US novelist.
Referring to *Uncle Tom's Cabin*

7 I started at the top and worked my way down.

Orson Welles (1915–85)
US film actor.

ADULTERY

1 It is better to be unfaithful than faithful without wanting to be.

Brigitte Bardot (1934–)
French film actress.

2 Sara could commit adultery at one end and weep for her sins at the other, and enjoy both operations at once.

Joyce Cary (1888–1957)
British novelist.

3 There were three of us in this marriage, so it was a bit crowded.

Diana, Princess of Wales (1961–97)
Former wife of Prince Charles.
On the relationship between her husband and Camilla Parker-Bowles

4 You know, of course, that the Tasmanians, who never committed adultery, are now extinct.

W. Somerset Maugham (1874–1965)
British novelist.

5 Madame, you must really be more careful. Suppose it had been someone else who found you like this.

Duc de Richelieu (1766–1822)
French statesman.
Discovering his wife with her lover

ADVICE

1 Advice is seldom welcome; and those who want it the most always like it the least.

Earl of Chesterfield (1694–1773)
English statesman.

2 I intended to give you some advice but now I remember how much is left over from last year unused.

George Harris (1844–1922)
US congressman.
Said when addressing students at the start of a new academic year

3 No one wants advice – only corroboration.

John Steinbeck (1902–68)
US novelist.

4 I have lived some thirty years on this planet, and I have yet to hear the first syllable of valuable or even earnest advice from my seniors.

Henry David Thoreau (1817–1862)
US writer.

AGE

1 Aging seems to be the only available way to live a long time.

Daniel-François-Esprit Auber (1782–1871)
French composer.

2 The only thing I regret about my past life is the length of it. If I had my past life over again I'd make all the same mistakes – only sooner.

Tallulah Bankhead (1903–68)
US actress.

3 What youth deemed crystal, age finds out was dew.

Robert Browning (1812–89)
British poet.

4 I was brought up to respect my elders and now I don't have to respect *anybody*.

George Burns (1896–1996)
US comedian.
Remark made at the age of 87

5 I prefer old age to the alternative.

Maurice Chevalier (1888–1972)
French singer and actor.

6 Oh to be seventy again.

Georges Clemenceau (1841–1929)
French statesman.
Remark on his eightieth birthday, noticing a pretty girl in the Champs Elysées

7 When a man fell into his anecdotage it was a sign for him to retire from the world.

Benjamin Disraeli (1804–81)
British statesman.

8 The years between fifty and seventy are the hardest. You are always being asked to do things, and you are not yet decrepit enough to turn them down.

T. S. Eliot (1888–1965)
US-born British poet and dramatist.

9   At sixteen I was stupid, confused, insecure and indecisive.
    At twenty-five I was wise, self-confident, prepossessing
    and assertive. At forty-five I am stupid, confused, insecure
    and indecisive. Who would have supposed that maturity is
    only a short break in adolescence?

Jules Feiffer (1929–)
US writer, cartoonist, and humorist.

10 He cannot bear old men's jokes. That is not new. But now
    he begins to think of them himself.

Max Frisch (1911–91)
Swiss dramatist and novelist.

11 A diplomat is a man who always remembers a woman's
    birthday but never remembers her age.

Robert Frost (1875–1963)
US poet.

12 A man is only as old as the woman he feels.

Groucho Marx (Julius Marx; 1895–1977)
US comedian.

13 From the earliest times the old have rubbed it into the
    young that they are wiser than they, and before the young
    had discovered what nonsense this was they were old too,
    and it profited them to carry on the imposture.

W. Somerset Maugham (1874–1965)
British novelist.

14 I prefer to forget both pairs of glasses and pass my

declining years saluting strange women and grandfather clocks.

Ogden Nash (1902–71)
US poet.

15 At 50, everyone has the face he deserves.

George Orwell (Eric Blair; 1903–50)
British novelist.
Last words in his manuscript notebook, 17 Apr 1949

16 Each generation imagines itself to be more intelligent than the one that went before it, and wiser than the one that comes after it.

George Orwell

17 Growing old is like being increasingly penalized for a crime you haven't committed.

Anthony Powell (1905–2000)
British novelist.

18 You know, by the time you reach my age, you've made plenty of mistakes if you've lived your life properly

Ronald Reagan (1911–)
US politician and president.

19 The young have aspirations that never come to pass, the old have reminiscences of what never happened.

Saki (Hector Hugh Munro; 1870–1916)
British writer.

20 When I was young, I was told: 'You'll see, when you're fifty'. I am fifty and I haven't seen a thing.

Erik Satie (1866–1925)
French composer.
From a letter to his brother

21 All that the young can do for the old is to shock them and keep them up to date.

George Bernard Shaw (1856–1950)
Irish dramatist and critic.

22 It's a funny thing about that bust. As time goes on it seems to get younger and younger.

George Bernard Shaw
Referring to a portrait bust sculpted for him by Rodin

23 Old men are dangerous; it doesn't matter to them what is going to happen to the world.

George Bernard Shaw

24 If you live long enough, the venerability factor creeps in; you get accused of things you never did and praised for virtues you never had.

I. F. Stone (1907–89)
US writer and publisher.

25 From birth to age eighteen, a girl needs good parents. From eighteen to thirty-five, she needs good looks. From thirty-five to fifty-five, she needs a good personality. From fifty-five on, she needs good cash.

Sophie Tucker (Sophia Abuza; 1884–1966)
Russian-born US singer.

AGREEMENT

1 When you say that you agree to a thing in principle you mean that you have not the slightest intention of carrying it out in practice.

Bismarck (1815–1898)
German statesman.

2   Whenever you accept our views we shall be in full
       agreement with you.

Moshe Dayan (1915–81)
Israeli general.
Said to the US statesman Cyrus Vance during Arab-Israeli negotiations

3   Our agenda is now exhausted. The secretary general is
       exhausted. All of you are exhausted. I find it comforting
       that, beginning with our very first day, we find ourselves
       in such complete unanimity.

Paul Henri Spaak (1899–1972)
Belgian statesman.
Concluding the first General Assembly meeting of the United Nations

4   Ah! don't say you agree with me. When people agree with
       me I always feel that I must be wrong.

Oscar Wilde (1854–1900)
Irish-born British dramatist.

AMBITION

1   Ah, but a man's reach should exceed his grasp,
       Or what's a heaven for?

Robert Browning (1812–89)
British poet.

2   If you would hit the mark, you must aim a little above it;
       Every arrow that flies feels the attraction of earth.

Henry Wadsworth Longfellow (1807–82)
US poet.

3   Fain would I climb, yet fear I to fall.

Walter Raleigh (1554–1618)
English explorer.
Written on a window pane with his diamond ring. He was alluding to

his relationship with Queen Elizabeth I, who wrote a reply underneath,
'If thy heart fails thee, climb not at all'.

4 Ambition often puts Men upon doing the meanest offices;
so climbing is performed in the same position with
creeping.

Jonathan Swift (1667–1745)
Irish-born Anglican priest and writer.

5 There is always room at the top.

Daniel Webster (1782–1852)
US statesman.
When advised not to become a lawyer because the profession was
overcrowded

AMERICA

1 America is the only nation in history which miraculously
has gone directly from barbarism to degeneration without
the usual interval of civilization.

Georges Clemenceau (1841–1929)
French statesman.
Attrib.

2 There is nothing wrong with America that cannot be
cured by what is right with America.

Bill Clinton (William Jefferson Clinton; 1946–)
US politician and president.

3 New York…that unnatural city where everyone is an
exile, none more so than the American.

Charlotte Perkins Gilman (1860–1935)
US writer.

4 America is a large, friendly dog in a very small room. Every time it wags its tail it knocks over a chair.

Arnold Toynbee (1890–1975)
British historian.

ANIMALS

1 I know two things about the horse,
And one of them is rather coarse.

Anonymous

2 Whenever you observe an animal closely, you feel as if a human being sitting inside were making fun of you.

Elias Canetti (1905–94)
Bulgarian-born novelist.

3 It takes a good deal of physical courage to ride a horse. This, however, I have. I get it at about forty cents a flask, and take it as required.

Stephen Leacock (1869–1944)
English-born Canadian economist and humorist.

4 To confess that you are totally Ignorant about the Horse, is social suicide: you will be despised by everybody, especially the horse.

W. C. Sellar (1898–1951)
British humorous writer.

5 Nowadays we don't think much of a man's love for an animal; we laugh at people who are attached to cats. But if we stop loving animals, aren't we bound to stop loving humans too?

Alexander Solzhenitsyn (1918–)
Russian novelist.

6   There are two things for which animals are to be envied:
they know nothing of future evils, or of what people say
about them.

Voltaire (François-Marie Arouet; 1694–1778)
French writer.

APOLOGIES

1   Very sorry can't come. Lie follows by post.

Charles Beresford (1846–1919)
British naval officer.
Reply, by telegram, to a dinner invitation at short notice from Edward,
Prince of Wales

2   Mr. Speaker, I said the honorable member was a liar it is
true and I am sorry for it. The honourable member may
place the punctuation where he pleases.

Richard Brinsley Sheridan (1751–1816)
British dramatist.
On being asked to apologize for calling a fellow MP a liar

3   It is a good rule in life never to apologize. The right sort
of people do not want apologies, and the wrong sort take
a mean advantage of them.

P. G. Wodehouse (1881–1975)
British humorous novelist.

APPEARANCE

1   It was a blonde. A blonde to make a bishop kick a hole in
a stained-glass window.

Raymond Chandler (1888–1959)
US novelist.

2   The most delightful advantage of being bald – one can hear snowflakes.

R. G. Daniels (1916–93)
British magistrate.

3   I am so changed that my oldest creditors would hardly know me.

Henry Stephen Fox (1791–1846)
British diplomat.
Remark after an illness

4   To see ourselves as others see us is a most salutary gift. Hardly less important is the capacity to see others as they see themselves.

Aldous Huxley (1894–1964)
British novelist.

5   The Lord prefers common-looking people. That is why he makes so many of them.

Abraham Lincoln (1809–65)
US statesman.

6   He looks as if he had been weaned on a pickle.

Alice Roosevelt Longworth (1884–1980)
US hostess.
Referring to John Calvin Coolidge, US president 1923–29

ARGUMENTS

1   Between friends differences in taste or opinion are irritating in direct proportion to their triviality.

W. H. Auden (1907–73)
British poet.

2   Never go to bed mad. Stay up and fight.

Phyllis Diller (1917–74)
US writer and comedienne.

3   One often contradicts an opinion when what is uncongenial is really the tone in which it was conveyed.

Friedrich Wilhelm Nietzsche (1844–1900)
German philosopher.

4   A man never tells you anything until you contradict him.

George Bernard Shaw (1856–1950)
Irish dramatist and critic.

5   I did not know that we had ever quarrelled.

Henry David Thoreau (1817–62)
US writer.
On being urged to make his peace with God

6   Arguments are to be avoided: they are always vulgar and often unconvincing.

Oscar Wilde (1854–1900)
Irish-born British dramatist.

ART

1   The object of art is to give life a shape.

Jean Anouilh (1910–87)
French dramatist

2   Remember I'm an artist. And you know what that means in a court of law. Next worst to an actress.

Joyce Cary (1888–1957)
British novelist

3 Buy old masters. They fetch a better price than old mistresses.

Lord Beaverbrook (1879–1964)
Canadian-born British newspaper proprietor.

4 Art is a jealous mistress.

Ralph Waldo Emerson (1803–82)
US poet and essayist.

5 The finest collection of frames I ever saw.

Humphry Davy (1778–1829)
British chemist.
When asked what he thought of the Paris art galleries

6 The trouble, Mr Goldwyn is that you are only interested in art and I am only interested in money.

George Bernard Shaw (1856–1950)
Irish dramatist and critic.
Turning down Goldwyn's offer to buy the screen rights of his plays

7 Skill without imagination is craftsmanship and gives us many useful objects such as wickerwork picnic baskets. Imagination without skill gives us modern art.

Tom Stoppard (1937–)
Czech-born British dramatist

AWARDS

1 I don't deserve this, but I have arthritis, and I don't deserve that either.

Jack Benny (Benjamin Kubelsky; 1894–1974)
US actor.
Said when accepting an award

2   When I want a peerage, I shall buy one like an honest
man.

Lord Northcliffe (1865–1922)
Irish-born British newspaper proprietor.

3   Mother always told me my day was coming, but I never
realized that I'd end up being the shortest knight of the
year.

Gordon Richards (1904–86)
British champion jockey.
Referring to his diminutive size, on hearing he had been awarded a
knighthood

BEAUTY

1   A thing of beauty is a joy for ever:
Its loveliness increases; it will never
Pass into nothingness; but still will keep
A bower quiet for us, and a sleep
Full of sweet dreams, and health, and quiet breathing.

John Keats (1795–1821)
British poet.

2   'Beauty is truth, truth beauty,' – that is all
Ye know on earth, and all ye need to know.

John Keats

3   Oh, thou art fairer than the evening air
Clad in the beauty of a thousand stars.

Christopher Marlowe (1564–93)
English dramatist.

4 Remember that the most beautiful things in the world are the most useless, peacocks and lilies for instance.

John Ruskin (1819–1900)
British art critic and writer.

5 I always say beauty is only sin deep.

Saki (Hector Hugh Munro; 1870–1916)
British writer.

BEGINNING

1 The distance doesn't matter; it is only the first step that is difficult.

Marquise du Deffand (Marie de Vichy-Chamrond; 1697–1780)
French noblewoman.
Referring to the legend of St Denis, who is traditionally believed to have carried his severed head for six miles after his execution

2 With the possible exception of the equator, everything begins somewhere.

Peter Fleming (1907–71)
British travel writer.

3 'Tis always morning somewhere in the world.

Richard Henry Horne (1803–84)
English writer.

BELIEF

1 A cause is like champagne and high heels – one must be prepared to suffer for it.

Arnold Bennett (1867–1931)
British novelist.

2 Vain are the thousand creeds
That move men's hearts: unutterably vain;
Worthless as wither'd weeds.

Emily Brontë (1818–48)
British novelist.

3 If Jesus Christ were to come to-day, people would not
even crucify him. They would ask him to dinner, and hear
what he had to say, and make fun of it.

Thomas Carlyle (1795–1881)
Scottish historian and essayist.

BETRAYAL

1 I hate the idea of causes, and if I had to choose between
betraying my country and betraying my friend, I hope I
should have the guts to betray my country.

E. M. Forster (1879–1970)
British novelist.

2 Treason doth never prosper: what's the reason?
For if it prosper, none dare call it treason.

John Harington (1561–1612)
English writer.

3 I'm waiting for the cock to crow.

William Morris Hughes (1864–1952)
Australian statesman.
Said in parliament, after being viciously critized by a member of his
own party

BOASTS

1 To give an accurate and exhaustive account of that period would need a far less brilliant pen than mine.

Max Beerbohm (1872–1956)
British writer.

2 I have done almost every human activity inside a taxi which does not require main drainage.

Alan Brien (1925–)
British critic.

3 All my shows are great. Some of them are bad. But they are all great.

Lew Grade (Lewis Winogradsky; 1906–98)
British film and TV producer.

4 I can piss the old boy in the snow.

Max Liebermann (1847–1935)
German painter.
Remark to an artist who said he could not draw General Paul von Hindenburg's face

5 I cannot tell you that, madam. Heaven has granted me no offspring.

James Whistler (1834–1903)
US painter.
Replying to a lady who had inquired whether he thought genius hereditary

6 Nothing, except my genius.

Oscar Wilde (1854–1900)
Irish-born British dramatist.
Replying to a US customs official on being asked if he had anything to declare

7 Who am I to tamper with a masterpiece?

Oscar Wilde
Refusing to make alterations to one of his own plays

8 And when we open our dykes, the waters are ten feet deep.

Wilhelmina (1880–1962)
Queen of the Netherlands.
Replying to a boast by Wilhelm II that his guardsmen were all seven feet tall

BOOKS

1 And further, by these, my son, be admonished: of making many books there is no end; and much study is a weariness of the flesh.

Bible: Ecclesiastes

2 A good book is the purest essence of a human soul.

Thomas Carlyle (1795–1881)
Scottish historian and essayist.
Speech made in support of the London Library

3 Learning hath gained most by those books by which the printers have lost.

Thomas Fuller (1608–61)
English historian.

4 A book may be amusing with numerous errors, or it may be very dull without a single absurdity.

Oliver Goldsmith (1728–74)
Irish-born British writer.

BOREDOM

1 Millions long for immortality who do not know what to do with themselves on a rainy Sunday afternoon.

Susan Ertz
British novelist and playwright.

2 The effect of boredom on a large scale in history is underestimated. It is a main cause of revolutions, and would soon bring to an end all the static Utopias and the farmyard civilization of the Fabians.

Dean Inge (1860–1954)
British churchman.

BUREAUCRACY

1 A memorandum is written not to inform the reader but to protect the writer.

Dean Acheson (1893–1971)
US lawyer and statesman.

2 I'm surprised that a government organization could do it that quickly.

Jimmy Carter (1924–)
US statesman.
Visiting Egypt, when told that it took twenty years to build the Great Pyramid

3 A committee is a cul-de-sac down which ideas are lured and then quietly strangled.

Barnett Cocks (1907–)
British political writer.

4 The number one book of the ages was written by a committee, and it was called The Bible.

Louis B. Mayer (1885–1957)
Russian-born US film producer.
Comment to writers who had objected to changes in their work

5 A government agency is the nearest thing to eternal life
we'll ever see on this earth.

Ronald Reagan (1911–)
US politician and president.

BUSINESS

1 You ask me what it is I do. Well actually, you know,
I'm partly a liaison man and partly P.R.O.
Essentially I integrate the current export drive
And basically I'm viable from ten o'clock till five.

John Betjeman (1906–84)
British poet.

2 Here's the rule for bargains: 'Do other men, for they
would do you'. That's the true business precept.

Charles Dickens (1812–70)
British novelist.

3 A business that makes nothing but money is a poor kind
of business.

Henry Ford (1863–1947)
US car manufacturer.

4 No nation was ever ruined by trade.

Benjamin Franklin (1706–90)
US scientist and statesman.

5 The salary of the chief executive of the large corporation
is not a market award for achievement. It is frequently in

the nature of a warm personal gesture by the individual to himself.

John Kenneth Galbraith (1908–)
US economist.

6 Where wealth and freedom reign, contentment fails,
And honour sinks where commerce long prevails.

Oliver Goldsmith (1728–74)
Irish-born British writer.

7 When you are skinning your customers, you should leave some skin on to grow so that you can skin them again.

Nikita Khrushchev (1894–1971)
Soviet statesman.
Said to British businessmen

8 He is the only man who is for ever apologizing for his occupation.

H. L. Mencken (1880–1956)
US journalist.
Referring to the businessman

9 The big print giveth and the fine print taketh away.

J. Fulton Sheen (1895–1979)
US Roman Catholic archbishop.
Referring to his contract for a television appearance

10 People of the same trade seldom meet together but the conversation ends in a conspiracy against the public, or in some diversion to raise prices.

Adam Smith (1723–90)
Scottish economist.

11 You never expected justice from a company, did you? They have neither a soul to lose nor a body to kick.

Sydney Smith (1771–1845)
British clergyman and essayist.

12 All business sagacity reduces itself in the last analysis to a judicious use of sabotage.

Thorstein Bunde Veblen (1857–1929)
US social scientist.

13 If Max gets to Heaven he won't last long. He will be chucked out for trying to pull off a merger between Heaven and Hell…after having secured a controlling interest in key subsidiary companies in both places, of course.

H. G. Wells (1866–1946)
British writer.
Referring to Lord Beaverbrook

14 Business underlies everything in our national life, including our spiritual life. Witness the fact that in the Lord's Prayer the first petition is for daily bread. No one can worship God or love his neighbour on an empty stomach.

Woodrow Wilson (1856–1925)
US statesman.

CENSORSHIP

1 Oh, I get it. PG means the hero gets the girl, 15 means the villain gets the girl – and 18 means that everybody gets the girl.

Michael Douglas (1944–)
US film star.
On British film ratings

2 Whenever books are burned men also in the end are burned.

Heinrich Heine (1797–1856)
German poet and writer.

3 Censorship is more depraving and corrupting than anything pornography can produce.

Tony Smythe (1938–)
Chairman of the National Council for Civil Liberties, Great Britain.

4 God forbid that any book should be banned. The practice is as indefensible as infanticide.

Rebecca West (Cicely Isabel Fairfield; 1892–1983)
British novelist and journalist.

CHANCE

1 When you take the bull by the horns... what happens is a toss up.

William Pett Ridge (1860–1930)
British novelist.

CHARACTER

1 It is with narrow-souled people as with narrow-necked bottles: the less they have in them, the more noise they make in pouring it out.

Alexander Pope (1688–1744)
British poet.

CHARITY

1 Don't bother to thank me. I know what a perfectly ghastly
season it's been for you Spanish dancers.

Tallulah Bankhead (1903–68)
US actress.
Said on dropping fifty dollars into a tambourine held out by a Salvation
Army collector

2 If you see anybody fallen by the wayside and lying in the
ditch, it isn't much good climbing into the ditch and lying
by his side.

H. R. L. Sheppard (1880–1937)
British clergyman.

3 To keep a lamp burning we have to keep putting oil in it.

Mother Teresa (Agnes Gonxha Bojaxhui; 1910–97)
Yugoslavian missionary in Calcutta.

CHARM

1 It's a sort of bloom on a woman. If you have it, you don't
need to have anything else; and if you don't have it, it
doesn't much matter what else you have.

J. M. Barrie (1860–1937)
British novelist and dramatist.

CHILDREN

1 Children have never been very good at listening to their
elders, but they have never failed to imitate them.

James Baldwin (1924–87)
US writer.

2 A woman when she is in travail hath sorrow, because her hour is come: but as soon as she is delivered of the child, she remembereth no more the anguish, for joy that a man is born into the world.

Bible: John

3 Boys do not grow up gradually. They move forward in spurts like the hands of clocks in railway stations.

Cyril Connolly (1903–74)
British journalist.

4 If men had to have babies they would only ever have one each.

Diana, Princess of Wales (1961–97)
Former wife of Prince Charles.

5 Every baby born into the world is a finer one than the last.

Charles Dickens (1812–70)
British novelist.

6 It is only rarely that one can see in a little boy the promise of a man, but one can almost always see in a little girl the threat of a woman.

Alexandre Dumas, fils (1824–95)
French writer.

7 A loud noise at one end and no sense of responsibility at the other.

Ronald Knox (1888–1957)
British Roman Catholic priest.

8 The baby doesn't understand English and the Devil knows Latin.

Ronald Knox

Said when asked to conduct a baptism service in English

9 Death and taxes and childbirth! There's never any convenient time for any of them!

Margaret Mitchell (1909–49)
US novelist.

10 Dear Mary, We all knew you had it in you.

Dorothy Parker (1893–1967)
US writer.

11 He that has no children brings them up well.

Proverb

12 There's only one pretty child in the world, and every mother has it.

Proverb

13 Parents learn a lot from their children about coping with life.

Muriel Spark (1918–)
British novelist.

14 Never have children, only grandchildren.

Gore Vidal (1925–)
US novelist.

CHIVALRY

1 A gentleman is any man who wouldn't hit a woman with his hat on.

Fred Allen (1894–1956)
US comedian.

2 Madame, I would have given you another!

Alfred Jarry (1873–1907)
French surrealist dramatist.
On being reprimanded by a woman for firing his pistol in the vicinity of
her child, who might have been killed

CHOICE

1 Two roads diverged in a wood, and I –
I took the one less traveled by,
And that has made all the difference.

Robert Frost (1875–1963)
US poet.

CIVILIZATION

1 Civilization is a method of living, an attitude of equal
respect for all men.

Jane Addams (1860–1935)
US social worker.

2 I think it would be a good idea.

Mahatma Gandhi (Mohandas Karamchand Gandhi; 1869–1948)
Indian national leader.
On being asked for his view on Western civilization

3 The degree of a nation's civilization is marked by its
disregard for the necessities of existence.

W. Somerset Maugham (1874–1965)
British novelist.

CLOTHES

1   I go to a better tailor than any of you and pay more for my clothes. The only difference is that you probably don't sleep in yours.

> **Clarence Seward Darrow** (1857–1938)
> US lawyer.
> Reply when teased by reporters about his appearance

2   How do you look when I'm sober?

> **Ring Lardner Jnr** (1885–1933)
> American humorist.
> Speaking to a flamboyantly dressed stranger who walked into the club where he was drinking

3   Brevity is the soul of lingerie.

> **Dorothy Parker** (1893–1967)
> US writer.

COMMUNISM

1   Capitalism is the exploitation of man by man.
Communism is the reverse.

> **Anonymous**
> Polish joke

2   Communism is like prohibition, it's a good idea but it won't work.

> **Will Rogers** (1879–1935)
> US actor and humorist.

COMPLAINTS

1   I want to register a complaint. Do you know who sneaked
    into my room at three o'clock this morning?...
    – Who?...
    Nobody, and that's my complaint.

    Groucho Marx (Julius Marx; 1895–1977)
    US comedian.

2   If this is the way Queen Victoria treats her prisoners, she
    doesn't deserve to have any.

    Oscar Wilde (1854–1900
    Irish-born British dramatist.
    Complaining at having to wait in the rain for transport to take him to
    prison

COMPLIMENTS

1   She walks in beauty, like the night
    Of cloudless climes and starry skies;
    And all that's best of dark and bright
    Meet in her aspect and her eyes.

    Lord Byron (1788–1824)
    British poet.

2   Your eyes shine like the pants of my blue serge suit.

    Groucho Marx (Julius Marx; 1895–1977)
    US comedian.

3   Age cannot wither her, nor custom stale
    Her infinite variety. Other women cloy
    The appetites they feed, but she makes hungry
    Where most she satisfies.

    William Shakespeare (1564–1616)
    English dramatist.

4   'A was a man, take him for all in all,
I shall not look upon his like again.

William Shakespeare

5   Shall I compare thee to a summer's day?
Thou art more lovely and more temperate.
Rough winds do shake the darling buds of May,
And summer's lease hath all too short a date.

William Shakespeare

6   Won't you come into the garden? I would like my roses to
see you.

Richard Brinsley Sheridan (1751–1816)
British dramatist.
Said to a young lady

7   She would rather light candles than curse the darkness,
and her glow has warmed the world.

Adlai Stevenson (1900–65)
US statesman.
Referring to Eleanor Roosevelt

8   What, when drunk, one sees in other women, one sees in
Garbo sober.

Kenneth Tynan (1927–80)
British theatre critic.

9   He was a great patriot, a humanitarian, a loyal friend –
provided, of course, that he really is dead.

Voltaire (François-Marie Arouet; 1694–1778)
French writer.
Giving a funeral oration

COMPROMISE

1 You cannot shake hands with a clenched fist.

Indira Gandhi (1917–84)
Indian stateswoman.

CONCEIT

1 No poet or novelist wishes he were the only one who ever lived, but most of them wish they were the only one alive, and quite a number fondly believe their wish has been granted.

W. H. Auden (1907–73)
British poet.

2 *Egotist,* n. A person of low taste, more interested in himself than in me.

Ambrose Bierce (1842–?1914)
US writer and journalist.

3 I know he is, and he adores his maker.

Benjamin Disraeli (1804–81)
British statesman.
Replying to a remark made in defence of John Bright that he was a self-made man; often also attrib. to Bright referring to Disraeli

CONFORMITY

1 Whoso would be a man must be a nonconformist.

Ralph Waldo Emerson (1803–82)
US poet and essayist.

2   Why do you have to be a nonconformist like everybody else?

> **James Thurber** (1894–1961)
> US humorist.
> Attrib. Actually a cartoon caption by Stan Hunt

CONSCIENCE

1   All a man can betray is his conscience.

> **Joseph Conrad** (Teodor Josef Konrad Korzeniowski; 1857–1924)
> Polish-born British novelist.

2   Conscience is the inner voice that warns us somebody may be looking.

> **H. I. Mencken** (1880–1956)
> US journalist.

CONTRACEPTION

1   Q. What do you call couples who use the rhythm method?
A. Parents.

> **Anonymous.**

2   I want to tell you a terrific story about oral contraception.
I asked this girl to sleep with me and she said 'no'.

> **Woody Allen** (Allen Stewart Konigsberg; 1935–)
> US film actor.

3   Contraceptives should be used on every conceivable occasion.

> **Spike Milligan** (1918–)
> British comic actor and author.

COURAGE

1 Because of my title, I was the first to enter here. I shall be the last to go out.

Duchesse d'Alençon (d. 1897)
Bavarian-born duchess.
Refusing help during a fire, 4 May 1897, at a charity bazaar in Paris.
She died along with 120 others.

2 If the creator had a purpose in equipping us with a neck, he surely meant us to stick it out.

Arthur Koestler (1905–83)
Hungarian-born British writer.

3 Let me assert my firm belief that the only thing we have to fear is fear itself.

Franklin D. Roosevelt (1882–1945)
US Democratic president.

4 He was a bold man that first eat an oyster.

Jonathan Swift (1667–1745)
Irish-born Anglican priest and writer.

CRIME

1 Thieves respect property; they merely wish the property to become their property that they may more perfectly respect it.

G. K. Chesterton (1874–1936)
British writer.
Attrib.

2   If poverty is the mother of crime, stupidity is its father.

Jean de La Bruyère (1645–96)
French satirist.

3   A man who has never gone to school may steal from a freight car, but if he has a university education he may steal the whole railroad.

Franklin D. Roosevelt (1882–1945)
US Democratic president.
Attrib.

CRITICISM

1   There is less in this than meets the eye.

Tallulah Bankhead (1903–68)
US actress.
Referring to a revival of a play by Maeterlinck

2   He played the King as though under momentary apprehension that someone else was about to play the ace.

Eugene Field (1850–95)
US poet and journalist.
Referring to Creston Clarke's performance in the role of King Lear

3   My dear chap! Good isn't the word!

W. S. Gilbert (1836–1911)
British dramatist.
Speaking to an actor after he had given a poor performance

4   We were as nearly bored as enthusiasm would permit.

Edmund Gosse (1849–1928)
British writer and critic.
Referring to a play by Swinburne

5 Difficult do you call it, Sir? I wish it were impossible.

Samuel Johnson (1709–84)
British lexicographer.
On hearing a famous violinist and being told that the piece played was difficult

6 A fly, Sir, may sting a stately horse and make him wince; but one is but an insect, and the other is a horse still.

Samuel Johnson (1709–84)
British lexicographer

7 From the moment I picked up your book until I laid it down, I was convulsed with laughter. Some day I intend reading it.

Groucho Marx (Julius Marx; 1895–1977)
US comedian and film actor.

8 Show me a critic without prejudices, and I'll show you an arrested cretin.

G. J. Nathan (1882–1958)
US theatre critic.

9 Your works will be read after Shakespeare and Milton are forgotten – and not till then.

Richard Porson (1759–1808)
British classicist.
Giving his opinion of the poems of Robert Southey

10 It had only one fault. It was kind of lousy.

James Thurber (1894–1961)
US humorist.
Remark made about a play

11   I do not think this poem will reach its
destination.

Voltaire (François-Marie Arouet; 1694–1778)
French writer.
Reviewing Rousseau's poem 'Ode to Posterity'

12   My dear fellow a unique evening! I wouldn't have left a
turn unstoned.

Arthur Wimperis (1874–1953)
British screenwriter.
Replying when asked his opinion of a vaudeville show

13   I saw it at a disadvantage – the curtain was up.

Walter Winchell (1879–1972)
US journalist.
Referring to a show starring Earl Carroll

CYNICISM

1   One is not superior merely because one sees the world in
an odious light.

Vicomte de Chateaubriand (1768–1848)
French diplomat and writer.

2   A man who knows the price of everything and the value
of nothing.

Oscar Wilde (1854–1900)
Irish-born British dramatist.

DEATH

1   It's not that I'm afraid to die. I just don't want to be there when it happens.

Woody Allen (Allen Stewart Konigsberg; 1935–)
US film actor.

2   I don't want to achieve immortality through my work…I want to achieve it through not dying.

Woody Allen

3   I have often thought upon death, and I find it the least of all evils.

Francis Bacon (1561–1626)
English philosopher.

4   It is important what a man still plans at the end. It shows the measure of injustice in his death.

Elias Canetti (1905–94)
Bulgarian-born novelist.

5   Death…It's the only thing we haven't succeeded in completely vulgarizing.

Aldous Huxley (1894–1964)
British novelist.

6   It matters not how a man dies, but how he lives. The act of dying is not of importance, it lasts so short a time.

Samuel Johnson (1709–84)
British lexicographer.

7   That is the road we all have to take – over the Bridge of Sighs into eternity.

Søren Kierkegaard (1813–55)
Danish philosopher.

8 Dying is a very dull, dreary affair. And my advice to you is to have nothing whatever to do with it.

W. Somerset Maugham (1874–1965)
British novelist.

9 Sleep after toil, port after stormy seas,
Ease after war, death after life does greatly please.

Edmund Spenser (1552–99)
English poet.

DEBAUCHERY

1 A great many people have come up to me and asked how I manage to get so much work done and still keep looking so dissipated.

Robert Benchley (1889–1945)
US humorist.

2 Home is heaven and orgies are vile
But you need an orgy once in a while.

Ogden Nash (1902–71)
US poet.

3 Once: a philosopher; twice: a pervert!

Voltaire (François-Marie Arouet; 1694–1778)
French writer.
Turning down an invitation to an orgy, having attended one the previous night for the first time

DECEPTION

1   Beware of false prophets, which come to you in sheep's clothing, but inwardly they are ravening wolves.

Bible: Matthew

2   You can fool some of the people all the time and all the people some of the time; but you can't fool all the people all the time.

Abraham Lincoln (1809–65)
US statesman.

3   You can fool too many of the people too much of the time.

James Thurber (1894–1961)
US humorist.

DEFEAT

1   As always, victory finds a hundred fathers, but defeat is an orphan.

Count Galeazzo Ciano (1903–44)
Italian foreign minister.

2   A man is not finished when he is defeated. He is finished when he quits.

Richard Milhous Nixon (1913–94)
US president.

3   If you're not big enough to lose, you're not big enough to win.

Walter Reutner (1907–70)
US trade-union leader.

DEMOCRACY

1   Democracy means government by discussion but it is only effective if you can stop people talking.

Clement Attlee (1883–1967)
British statesman and Labour prime minister.

2   Democracy means government by the uneducated, while aristocracy means government by the badly educated.

G. K. Chesterton (1874–1936)
British writer.

3   Democracy means choosing your dictators, after they've told you what it is you want to hear.

Alan Coren (1938–)
British humorist and writer.

4   The theory that common people know what they want, and deserve to get it good and hard.

H. L. Mencken (1880–1956)
US journalist.

5   All the ills of democracy can be cured by more democracy.

Al Smith (1873–1944)
US politician.

6   It's not the voting that's democracy; it's the counting.

Tom Stoppard (1937–)
Czech-born British dramatist.

DESTINY

1   The Moving Finger writes; and, having writ,

Moves on: nor all thy Piety nor Wit
Shall lure it back to cancel half a Line,
Nor all thy Tears wash out a Word of it.

Edward Fitzgerald (1809–83)
British poet.

DIPLOMACY

1   It is better for aged diplomats to be bored than for young
men to die.

Warren Austin (1877–1962)
US politician and diplomat.
When asked if he got tired during long debates at the UN

2   An appeaser is one who feeds a crocodile – hoping that it
will eat him last.

Winston Churchill (1874–1965)
British statesman.

3   The art of dividing a cake in such a way that everyone
believes he has the biggest piece.

Ludwig Erhard (1897–1977)
German politician.

4   A real diplomat is one who can cut his neighbour's throat
without having his neighbour notice it.

Tryggve Lie (1896–1968)
Former secretary-general of the United Nations.

5   A diplomat these days is nothing but a head-waiter who's
allowed to sit down occasionally.

Peter Ustinov (1921–)
British actor

6 An ambassador is an honest man sent to lie abroad for the good of his country.

Henry Wotton (1568–1639)
English poet and diplomat.

DISCOVERY

1 None of the great discoveries was made by a 'specialist' or a 'researcher'.

Martin J. Fischer (1879–1962)

2 Discovery consists of seeing what everybody has seen and thinking what nobody has thought.

Albert Szent-Györgyi (1893–1986)
Hungarian-born US biochemist.

DOGS

1 The great pleasure of a dog is that you may make a fool of yourself with him and not only will he not scold you, he will make a fool of himself too.

Samuel Butler (1835–1902)
British writer.

2 A door is what a dog is perpetually on the wrong side of.

Ogden Nash (1902–71)
US poet.

3 I loathe people who keep dogs. They are cowards who haven't got the guts to bite people themselves.

August Strindberg (1849–1912)
Swedish dramatist.

DOUBT

1   The trouble with the world is that the stupid are cocksure and the intelligent full of doubt.

Bertrand Russell (1872–1970)
British philosopher.

DRINKING

1   If all be true that I do think,
There are five reasons we should drink;
Good wine – a friend – or being dry –
Or lest we should be by and by –
Or any other reason why.

Dean Aldrich (1647–1710)
English poet.

2   One reason I don't drink is that I want to know when I am having a good time.

Nancy Astor (1879–1964)
American-born British politician.

3   So who's in a hurry?

Robert Benchley (1889–1945)
US humorist.
When asked whether he knew that drinking was a slow death

4   Drink no longer water, but use a little wine for thy stomach's sake and thine often infirmities.

Bible: I Timothy

5   Alcohol is like love: the first kiss is magic, the second is intimate, the third is routine. After that you just take the girl's clothes off.

Raymond Chandler (1888–1959)
US novelist.

6 If you believe Cratinus from days of old, Maecenas, (as you must know) no verse can give pleasure for long, nor last, that is written by drinkers of water.

Horace (Quintus Horatius Flaccus; 65–8 BC)
Roman poet.

7 Malt does more than Milton can
To justify God's ways to man.

A. E. Housman (1859–1936)
British scholar and poet.

8 A tavern chair is the throne of human felicity.

Samuel Johnson (1709–84)
British lexicographer.

9 There is nothing which has yet been contrived by man, by which so much happiness is produced as by a good tavern or inn.

Samuel Johnson

10 Even though a number of people have tried, no one has yet found a way to drink for a living.

Jean Kerr (1923–)
US dramatist.

11 I drink for the thirst to come.

François Rabelais (1483–1553)
French satirist.

12 I am as drunk as a lord, but then, I am one, so what does it matter?

Bertrand Russell (1872–1970)
British philosopher.

13 People may say what they like about the decay of Christianity; the religious system that produced green Chartreuse can never really die.

Saki (Hector Hugh Munro; 1870–1916)
British writer.

14 It provokes the desire, but it takes away the performance. Therefore much drink may be said to be an equivocator with lechery.

William Shakespeare (1564–1616)
English dramatist.

15 Alcohol is a very necessary article...It enables Parliament to do things at eleven at night that no sane person would do at eleven in the morning.

George Bernard Shaw (1856–1950)
Irish dramatist and critic.

16 If I had all the money I've spent on drink, I'd go out and spend it on drink.

Vivian Stanshall (1943–95)
British rock musician and humorist.

17 I hadn't the heart to touch my breakfast. I told Jeeves to drink it himself.

P. G. Wodehouse (1881–1975)
British humorous novelist.

DUTY

1 Do your duty and leave the rest to the Gods.

Pierre Corneille (1606–84)
French dramatist.

2 She's the sort of woman who lives for others – you can always tell the others by their hunted expression.

C. S. Lewis (1898–1963)
British academic and writer.

ECONOMICS

1 The one profession where you can gain great eminence without ever being right.

George Meany (1894–1980)
US trade-union leader.
On economists

2 Recession is when a neighbour loses his job; depression is when you lose yours.

Ronald Reagan (1911–)
US politician and president.

3 If all economists were laid end to end, they would not reach a conclusion.

George Bernard Shaw (1856–1950)
Irish dramatist and critic.

4 Give me a one-handed economist! All my economists say, 'on the one hand…on the other.'

Harry S. Truman (1884–1972)
US politician and president.

EDUCATION

1   Miss not the discourse of the elders: for they also learned of their fathers, and of them thou shalt learn understanding, and to give answer as need requireth.

Bible: Ecclesiasticus

2   *Brain,* n. An apparatus with which we think that we think.

Ambrose Bierce (1842–?1914)
US writer and journalist.

3   Education is simply the soul of a society as it passes from one generation to another.

G. K. Chesterton (1874–1936)
British writer.

4   Examinations are formidable even to the best prepared, for the greatest fool may ask more than the wisest man can answer.

Charles Caleb Colton (?1780–1832)
British clergyman and writer.

5   We know the human brain is a device to keep the ears from grating on one another.

Peter De Vries (1910–93)
US novelist.

6   When a man's education is finished, he is finished.

E. A. Filene (1860–1937)
US financier.

7   Spoon feeding in the long run teaches us nothing but the shape of the spoon.

E. M. Forster (1879–1970)
British novelist.

8   …that is what learning is. You suddenly understand
something you've understood all your life, but in a new
way.

Doris Lessing (1919–)
British novelist.

9   A man who has never gone to school may steal from a
freight car, but if he has a university education he may
steal the whole railroad.

Franklin D. Roosevelt (1882–1945)
US Democratic president.

10   There is nothing on earth intended for innocent people so
horrible as a school. It is in some respects more cruel
than a prison. In a prison, for example, you are not forced
to read books written by the warders and the governor.

George Bernard Shaw (1856–1950)
Irish dramatist and critic.

11   Education is what survives when what has been learnt
has been forgotten.

B. F. Skinner (1904–90)
US psychologist.

12   I have never let my schooling interfere with my
education.

Mark Twain (Samuel Langhorne Clemens; 1835–1910)
US writer.

13   Anyone who has been to an English public school will
always feel comparatively at home in prison.

Evelyn Waugh (1903–66)
British novelist.

14   Education is an admirable thing, but it is well to remember from time to time that nothing that is worth knowing can be taught.

Oscar Wilde (1854–1900)
Irish-born British dramatist.

ENDURANCE

1   …we could never learn to be brave and patient, if there were only joy in the world.

Helen Keller (1880–1968)
US writer and lecturer.

2   No pain, no palm; no thorns, no throne; no gall, no glory; no cross, no crown.

William Penn (1644–1718)
English preacher.

3   The pain passes, but the beauty remains.

Pierre Auguste Renoir (1841–1919)
French impressionist painter.
Explaining why he still painted when his hands were twisted with arthritis

4   Does the road wind up-hill all the way?
Yes, to the very end.
Will the day's journey take the whole long day?
From morn to night, my friend.

Christina Rossetti (1830–74)
British poet.

5   For there was never yet philosopher
That could endure the toothache patiently.

William Shakespeare (1564–1616)
English dramatist.

6   Maybe one day we shall be glad to remember even these
hardships.

Virgil (Publius Vergilius Maro; 70–19 BC)
Roman poet.

ENEMIES

1   Always forgive your enemies – but never forget their
names.

Robert Kennedy (1925–68)
US politician.

2   Even a paranoid can have enemies.

Henry Kissinger (1923–)
German-born US politician and diplomat.

3   You must despise your enemy strategically, but respect
him tactically.

Mao Tse-Tung (1893–1976)
Chinese communist leader.

4   It takes your enemy and your friend, working together, to
hurt you to the heart; the one to slander you and the
other to get the news to you.

Mark Twain (Samuel Langhorne Clemens; 1835–1910)
US writer.

ENGLAND

1 England is a paradise for women, and hell for horses: Italy a paradise for horses, hell for women.

Robert Burton (1577–1640)
English scholar and explorer.

2 There are many things in life more worthwhile than money. One is to be brought up in this our England which is still the envy of less happy lands.

Lord Denning (1899–1999)
British judge.

3 …the English think of an opinion as something which a decent person, if he has the misfortune to have one, does all he can to hide.

Margaret Halsey (1910–97)
US writer.

4 England is…a country infested with people who love to tell us what to do, but who very rarely seem to know what's going on.

Colin MacInnes (1914–76)
British novelist.

5 An Englishman, even if he is alone, forms an orderly queue of one.

George Mikes (1912–87)
Hungarian-born British writer.

6 Continental people have sex life; the English have hot-water bottles.

George Mikes

7 Remember that you are an Englishman, and have

consequently won first prize in the lottery
of life.

Cecil Rhodes (1853–1902)
South African statesman.

8 The English have no respect for their language, and will
not teach their children to speak it…It is impossible for
an Englishman to open his mouth, without making some
other Englishman despise him.

George Bernard Shaw (1856–1950)
Irish dramatist and critic.

9 The English take their pleasures sadly after the fashion of
their country.

Duc de Sully (1560–1641)
French statesman.

10 Men of England! You wish to kill me because I am a
Frenchman. Am I not punished enough in not being born
an Englishman?

Voltaire (François-Marie Arouet; 1694–1778)
French writer.
Addressing an angry London mob who desired to hang him because
he was a Frenchman

11 You never find an Englishman among the underdogs –
except in England of course.

Evelyn Waugh (1903–66)
British novelist.

ENTHUSIASM

1 Nothing great was ever achieved without enthusiasm.

Ralph Waldo Emerson (1803–82)
US poet and essayist.

ENVY

1 The man with toothache thinks everyone happy whose teeth are sound.

George Bernard Shaw (1856–1950)
Irish dramatist and critic.

EQUALITY

1 The majestic egalitarianism of the law, which forbids rich and poor alike to sleep under bridges, to beg in the streets, and to steal bread.

Anatole France (Jacques Anatole François Thibault; 1844–1924)
French writer.

2 Your levellers wish to level *down* as far as themselves; but they cannot bear levelling *up* to themselves.

Samuel Johnson (1709–84)
British lexicographer.

3 All men are born equal, but quite a few get over it.

Lord Mancroft (1917–87)
British businessman and writer.

4 In heaven an angel is nobody in particular.

George Bernard Shaw (1856–1950)
Irish dramatist and critic.

5 Everybody should have an equal chance – but they shouldn't have a flying start.

Harold Wilson (1916–95)
British politician and prime minister.

EVIL

1   The fearsome word-and-thought-defying *banality of evil*.

Hannah Arendt (1906–75)
German-born US philosopher and historian.

2   He who passively accepts evil is as much involved in it as he who helps to perpetrate it.

Martin Luther King (1929–68)
US Black civil-rights leader.

3   There is scarcely a single man sufficiently aware to know all the evil he does.

Duc de Rochefoucauld (1613–80)
French writer.

EXCESS

1   In baiting a mouse-trap with cheese, always leave room for the mouse.

Saki (Hector Hugh Munro; 1870–1916)
British writer.

2   Moderation is a fatal thing, Lady Hunstanton. Nothing succeeds like excess.

Oscar Wilde (1854–1900)
Irish-born British dramatist.

EXCUSES

1   Nothing grows well in the shade of a big tree.

Constantin Brancusi (1876–1957)
Romanian sculptor.
Refusing Rodin's invitation to work in his studio

2   Thank you for the manuscript; I shall lose no time in reading it.

> **Benjamin Disraeli** (1804–81)
> British statesman.
> His customary reply to those who sent him unsolicited manuscripts

3   When a stupid man is doing something he is ashamed of, he always declares that it is his duty.

> **George Bernard Shaw** (1856–1950)
> Irish dramatist and critic.

EXPERIENCE

1   One should try everything once, except incest and folk-dancing.

> **Arnold Bax** (1883–1953)
> British composer.

EXPERTS

1   An expert is a man who has made all the mistakes, which can be made, in a very narrow field.

> **Niels Bohr** (1885–1962)
> Danish physicist.

2   Specialist – A man who knows more and more about less and less.

> **William James Mayo** (1861–1934)
> US surgeon.

FACTS

1   Facts are not science – as the dictionary is not literature.

Martin H. Fischer (1879–1962)

2   Facts are ventriloquists' dummies. Sitting on a wise man's knee they may be made to utter words of wisdom; elsewhere they say nothing or talk nonsense.

Aldous Huxley (1894–1964)
British novelist.

FAILURE

1   The best laid schemes o' mice an' men
Gang aft a-gley,
An' lea'e us nought but grief an' pain
For promis'd joy.

Robert Burns (1759–96)
Scottish poet.

2   He said that he was too old to cry, but it hurt too much to laugh.

Adlai Stevenson (1900–65)
US statesman.
Said after losing an election, quoting a story told by Abraham Lincoln

3   Well, I have one consolation, No candidate was ever elected ex-president by such a large majority!

William Howard Taft (1857–1930)
US statesman.
Referring to his disastrous defeat in the 1912 presidential election

FAITH

1 I feel no need for any other faith than my faith in human beings.

Pearl Buck (1892–1973)
US novelist.

2 My dear child, you must believe in God in spite of what the clergy tell you.

Benjamin Jowett (1817–93)
British theologian.

3 'Tis not the dying for a faith that's so hard, Master Harry – every man of every nation has done that – 'tis the living up to it that is difficult.

William Makepeace Thackeray (1811–63)
British novelist.

FAME

1 A celebrity is a person who works hard all his life to become known, then wears dark glasses to avoid being recognized.

Fred Allen (1894–1956)
US comedian.

2 Being a star has made it possible for me to get insulted in places where the average Negro could never hope to get insulted.

Sammy Davis Jnr (1925–90)
Black US singer.

3 The nice thing about being a celebrity is that when you bore people, they think it's their fault.

Henry Kissinger (1923–)
German-born US politician and diplomat.

4   If you have to tell them who you are, you aren't anybody.

Gregory Peck (1916–)
US film star.
Remarking upon the failure of anyone in a crowded restaurant to recognize him

FAMILY

1   If one is not going to take the necessary precautions to avoid having parents one must undertake to bring them up.

Quentin Crisp (c. 1910–99)
British model, publicist, and writer.

2   Keeping up with the Joneses was a full-time job with my mother and father. It was not until many years later when I lived alone that I realized how much cheaper it was to drag the Joneses down to my level.

Quentin Crisp

3   Fate chooses your relations, you choose your friends.

Jacques Delille (1738–1813)
French abbé and poet.

4   You're a disgrace to our family name of Wagstaff, if such a thing is possible.

Groucho Marx (Julius Marx; 1895–1977)
US comedian.

5   No matter how many communes anybody invents, the family always creeps back.

Margaret Mead (1901–78)
US anthropologist.

6 Parents are sometimes a bit of a disappointment to their children. They don't fulfil the promise of their early years.

Anthony Powell (1905–2000)
British novelist.

7 It is a wise father that knows his own child.

William Shakespeare (1564–1616)
English dramatist.

8 No man is responsible for his father. That is entirely his mother's affair.

Margaret Turnbull (fl. 1920s–1942)
US writer.

9 Don't hold your parents up to contempt. After all, you are their son, and it is just possible that you may take after them.

Evelyn Waugh (1903–66)
British novelist.

10 The thing that impresses me most about America is the way parents obey their children.

Duke of Windsor (1894–1972)
King of the United Kingdom; abdicated 1936.

FASHION

1 One had as good be out of the world, as out of the fashion.

Colley Cibber (1671–1757)
British actor and dramatist.

2 Her frocks are built in Paris but she wears them with a strong English accent.

Saki (Hector Hugh Munro; 1870–1916)
British writer.

3 For an idea ever to be fashionable is ominous, since it must afterwards be always old-fashioned.

George Santayana (1863–1952)
US philosopher.

FEMINISM

1 I'm furious about the Women's Liberationists. They keep getting up on soapboxes and proclaiming that women are brighter than men. That's true, but it should be kept very quiet or it ruins the whole racket.

Anita Loos (1891–1981)
US novelist.

2 People call me a feminist whenever I express sentiments that differentiate me from a doormat or a prostitute.

Rebecca West (Cicely Isabel Fairfield; 1892–1983)
British novelist and journalist.
Attrib.

3 WOMEN'S RIGHTS NOW!
Followed by
YES DEAR

Exchange of graffiti

FLATTERY

1   A rich man's joke is always funny.

> **Thomas Edward Brown** (1830–97)
> British poet.

2   It is always pleasant to be urged to do something on the ground that one can do it well.

> **George Santayana** (1863–1952)
> US philosopher.

3   Flattery is all right so long as you don't inhale.

> **Adlai Stevenson** (1900–65)
> US statesman.
> Attrib.

FOOD

1   A good eater must be a good man; for a good eater must have a good digestion, and a good digestion depends upon a good conscience.

> **Benjamin Disraeli, Lord Beaconsfield** (1804–81)
> British statesman.

2   Food is an important part of a balanced diet.

> **Fran Lebowitz** (1950–)
> US writer.

3   Dinner at the Huntercombes' possessed 'only two dramatic features – the wine was a farce and the food a tragedy'.

> **Anthony Powell** (1905–2000)
> British novelist.

FREEDOM

1   My people and I have come to an agreement which
    satisfies us both. They are to say what they please, and I
    am to do what I please.

    Frederick the Great (1712–86)
    King of Prussia.

2   I have got no further than this: Every man has a right to
    utter what he thinks truth, and every other man has a
    right to knock him down for it. Martyrdom is the test.

    Samuel Johnson (1709–84)
    British lexicographer.

3   It's often safer to be in chains than to be free.

    Franz Kafka (1883–1924)
    Czech novelist.

4   Freedom's just another word for nothing left to lose.

    Kris Kristofferson (1936–)
    US film actor and folk musician.

5   Freedom is the right to tell people what they do not want
    to hear.

    George Orwell (Eric Blair; 1903–50)
    British novelist.

6   We have to believe in free will. We've got no choice.

    Isaac Bashevis Singer (1904–91)
    Polish-born US writer.

7   A free society is a society where it is safe to be unpopular.

    Adlai Stevenson (1900–65)
    US statesman.

8   It is by the goodness of God that in our country we have those three unspeakably precious things: freedom of speech, freedom of conscience, and the prudence never to practise either of them.

Mark Twain (Samuel Langhorne Clemens; 1835–1910)
US writer.

9   I disapprove of what you say, but I will defend to the death your right to say it.

Voltaire (François-Marie Arouet; 1694–1778)
French writer.

FRIENDSHIP

1   Forsake not an old friend; for the new is not comparable to him: a new friend is as new wine; when it is old, thou shalt drink it with pleasure.

Bible: Ecclesiasticus

2   But of all plagues, good Heaven, thy wrath can send,
Save me, oh save me, from the candid friend.

George Canning (1770–1827)
British statesman.

3   Two may talk together under the same roof for many years, yet never really meet; and two others at first speech are old friends.

Mary Catherwood (1847–1901)
US writer.

4   There is nothing in the world I wouldn't do for Hope, and there is nothing he wouldn't do for me…We spend our lives doing nothing for each other.

Bing Crosby (Harry Lillis Crosby; 1904–77)
US singer.
Referring to Bob Hope

5 Instead of loving your enemies, treat your friends a little better.

E. W. Howe (1853–1937)
US novelist.

6 Sir, I look upon every day to be lost, in which I do not make a new acquaintance.

Samuel Johnson (1709–84)
British lexicographer.

7 Men seem to kick friendship around like a football, but it doesn't seem to crack. Women treat it as glass and it goes to pieces.

Anne Morrow Lindbergh (1906–)
US poet.

8 Love is blind; friendship closes its eyes.

Proverb

9 So long as we are loved by others I should say that we are almost indispensable; and no man is useless while he has a friend.

Robert Louis Stevenson (1850–94)
Scottish writer.

10 Such a good friend that she will throw all her acquaintances into the water for the pleasure of fishing them out again.

Talleyrand (Charles Maurice de Talleyrand-Périgord; 1754–1838)
French politician.
Referring to Madame de Staël

11   Whenever a friend succeeds, a little something in me dies.

Gore Vidal (1925–)
US novelist.

12   We cherish our friends not for their ability to amuse us, but for ours to amuse them.

Evelyn Waugh (1903–66)
British novelist.

FUNERALS

1   This is the last time that I will take part as an amateur.

Daniel-François-Esprit Auber (1782–1871)
French composer.
Said at a funeral

2   Stop all the clocks, cut off the telephone,
Prevent the dog from barking with a juicy bone,
Silence the pianos and with muffled drum
Bring out the coffin, let the mourners come.

W. H. Auden (1907–73)
British poet.

3   'If you don't go to other men's funerals,' he told Father stiffly, 'they won't go to yours.'

Clarence Shepard Day (1874–1935)
US writer.

4   I bet you a hundred bucks he ain't in here.

Charles Bancroft Dillingham (1868–1934)
US theatrical manager.
Referring to the escapologist Harry Houdini; said at his funeral, while carrying his coffin

5   When I die I want to decompose in a barrel of porter and have it served in all the pubs in Dublin.

J. P. Donleavy (1926–)
US novelist.

6   It proves what they say, give the public what they want to see and they'll come out for it.

Red Skelton (Richard Bernard Skelton; 1913–97)
US actor and comedian.
Said while attending the funeral in 1958 of Hollywood producer Harry Cohn. It has also been attributed to Samuel Goldwyn while attending Louis B. Mayer's funeral in 1957

FUTURE

1   Boast not thyself of tomorrow; for thou knowest not what a day may bring forth.

Bible: Proverbs

2   *Future*, n. That period of time in which our affairs prosper, our friends are true and our happiness is assured.

Ambrose Bierce (1842–?1914)
US writer.

3   I never think of the future. It comes soon enough.

Albert Einstein (1879–1955)
German-born US physicist.

4   I have seen the future and it works.

Lincoln Steffens (1866–1936)
US journalist.
Speaking to Bernard Baruch after visiting the
Soviet Union, 1919

5   The future is made of the same stuff as the present.

Simone Weil (1909–43)
French philosopher.

GAMES

1   It is very wonderful to see persons of the best sense
passing away a dozen hours together in shuffling and
dividing a pack of cards, with no other conversation but
what is made up of a few game phrases, and no other
ideas but those of black or red spots ranged together in
different figures.

Joseph Addison (1672–1719)
British essayist.

2   Life's too short for chess.

Henry James Byron (1834–84)
British dramatist and actor.

3   I am still a victim of chess. It has all the beauty of art –
and much more. It cannot be commercialized. Chess is
much purer than art in its social position.

Marcel Duchamp (1887–1968)
French artist.

4   A man's idea in a card game is war – cool, devastating and
pitiless. A lady's idea of it is a combination of larceny,
embezzlement and burglary.

Finley Peter Dunne (1867–1936)
US journalist.

5   I am sorry I have not learned to play at cards. It is very useful in life: it generates kindness and consolidates society.

Samuel Johnson (1709–84)
British lexicographer.

GENERALIZATIONS

1   All generalizations are dangerous, even this one.

Alexandre Dumas, fils (1824–95)
French writer.

GIFTS

1   The manner of giving is worth more than the gift.

Pierre Corneille (1606–84)
French dramatist.

GOD

1   A God who let us prove his existence would be an idol.

Dietrich Bonhoeffer (1906–45)
German theologian.

2   Thou shalt have one God only; who
Would be at the expense of two?

Arthur Hugh Clough (1819–61)
British poet.

GOLDWYNISMS

1   Too caustic? To hell with cost; we'll make the picture anyway.

2   We're overpaying him but he's worth it.

3   I am willing to admit that I may not always be right, but I am never wrong.

4   Anybody who goes to see a psychiatrist ought to have his head examined.

5   I'll give you a definite maybe.

6   A verbal contract isn't worth the paper it's written on.

7   We have all passed a lot of water since then.

8   Tell me, how did you love my picture?

GOOD

1   He who would do good to another must do it in Minute Particulars.
General Good is the plea of the scoundrel, hypocrite, and flatterer.

William Blake (1757–1827)
British poet and painter.

2   Evil comes at leisure like the disease; good comes in a hurry like the doctor.

G. K. Chesterton (1874–1936)
British writer.

3   What is a weed? A plant whose virtues have not been discovered.

Ralph Waldo Emerson (1803–82)
US poet and essayist.

4   Do good by stealth, and blush to find it fame.

Alexander Pope (1688–1744)
British poet.

5   How far that little candle throws his beams!
So shines a good deed in a naughty world.

William Shakespeare (1564–1616)
English dramatist.

6   Nothing can harm a good man, either in life or after
death.

Socrates (469–399 BC)
Athenian philosopher.

7   – My goodness those diamonds are lovely!
Goodness had nothing whatever to do with it.

Mae West (1892–1980)
US actress.
Used in 1959 as the title of the first volume of her autobiography

GOSSIP

1   No one gossips about other people's secret virtues.

Bertrand Russell (1872–1970)
British philosopher.

GOVERNMENT

1   One day the don't-knows will get in, and then where will
we be?

Spike Milligan (1918–)
British comic actor and author.

2 I don't make jokes. I just watch the government and report the facts.

Will Rogers (1879–1935)
US actor and humorist.

3 Parliament is the longest running farce in the West End.

Cyril Smith (1928–93)
British Liberal politician.

GREATNESS

1 No great man lives in vain. The history of the world is but the biography of great men.

Thomas Carlyle (1795–1881)
Scottish historian and essayist.

2 To be great is to be misunderstood.

Ralph Waldo Emerson (1803–82)
US poet and essayist.

GREED

1 Gluttony is an emotional escape, a sign something is eating us.

Peter De Vries (1910–93)
US novelist.

2 Wealth is like sea-water; the more we drink, the thirstier we become; and the same is true of fame.

Arthur Schopenhauer (1788–1860)
German philosopher.

HAPPINESS

1   Ask yourself whether you are happy, and you cease to be so.

John Stuart Mill (1806–73)
British philosopher.

2   When a small child…I thought that success spelled happiness. I was wrong. Happiness is like a butterfly which appears and delights us for one brief moment, but soon flits away.

Anna Pavlova (1881–1931)
Russian ballet dancer.

3   To be without some of the things you want is an indispensable part of happiness.

Bertrand Russell (1872–1970)
British philosopher.

4   Happiness? That's nothing more than health and a poor memory.

Albert Schweitzer (1875–1950)
French Protestant theologian, philosopher, physician, and musician.

5   Happiness is an imaginary condition, formerly often attributed by the living to the dead, now usually attributed by adults to children, and by children to adults.

Thomas Szasz (1920–)
US psychiatrist.

6   Happiness is no laughing matter.

Richard Whately (1787–1863)
British churchman.

HASTE

1 In skating over thin ice, our safety is in our speed.

Ralph Waldo Emerson (1803–82)
US poet and essayist.

HATE

1 I am free of all prejudice. I hate everyone equally.

W. C. Fields (1880–1946)
US actor.

2 Few people can be happy unless they hate some other person, nation or creed.

Bertrand Russell (1872–1970)
British philosopher.

HEALTH AND HEALTHY LIVING

1 Vegetarianism is harmless enough, though it is apt to fill a man with wind and self righteousness.

Robert Hutchinson (1871–1960)
British medical writer.

2 Sickness is felt, but health not at all.

Proverb

3 A substance that makes you ill if you don't eat it.

Albert von Szent-Györgi (1893–1986)
Hungarian-born US biochemist.
His definition of a vitamin

4 Early to rise and early to bed makes a male healthy and wealthy and dead.

James Thurber (1894–1961)
US humorist.

HISTORY

1 History…records the names of royal bastards, but cannot tell us the origin of wheat.

Jean Henri Fabre (1823–1915)
French entomologist.

2 History never looks like history when you are living through it. It always looks confusing and messy, and it always feels uncomfortable.

John W. Gardner (1912–)
US writer.

3 Events in the past may roughly be divided into those which probably never happened and those which do not matter.

Dean Inge (1860–1954)
British churchman.

HOME

1 The house is well, but it is you, Your Majesty, who have made me too great for my house.

Francis Bacon (1561–1626)
English philosopher.
Reply when Elizabeth I remarked on the smallness of his house

2   Home is the place where, when you have to go there,
They have to take you in.

Robert Frost (1875–1963)
US poet.

3   A man travels the world over in search of what he needs
and returns home to find it.

George Moore (1852–1933)
Irish writer and art critic.

4   Home is where you go when you have nothing else to do.

Margaret Thatcher (1925–)
British politician and prime minister.

HONESTY

1   Honesty is the best policy; but he who is governed by that
maxim is not an honest man.

Richard Whately (1787–1863)
British churchman.

HONOUR

1   Remember, men, we're fighting for this woman's honour;
which is probably more than she ever did.

Groucho Marx (Julius Marx; 1895–1977)
US comedian.

HOSPITALITY

1   Let brotherly love continue.
Be not forgetful to entertain strangers: for thereby some
have entertained angels unawares.

Bible: Hebrews

2 A constant guest is never welcome.

Proverb

HOUSES OF PARLIAMENT

1 The House of Lords is like a glass of champagne that has stood for five days.

Clement Attlee (1883–1967)
British statesman and Labour prime minister.

2 A severe though not unfriendly critic of our institutions said that 'the cure for admiring the House of Lords was to go and look at it.'

Walter Bagehot (1826–77)
British economist and journalist.

3 The House of Lords is a model of how to care for the elderly.

Frank Field (1942–)
British politician.

4 Every man has a House of Lords in his own head. Fears, prejudices, misconceptions – those are the peers, and they are hereditary.

David Lloyd George (1863–1945)
British Liberal statesman.

5 The House of Lords must be the only institution in the world which is kept efficient by the persistent absenteeism of most of its members.

Herbert Samuel (1870–1963)
British Liberal statesman.

HUMAN NATURE

1 Upon the whole I dislike mankind: whatever people on the other side of the question may advance, they cannot deny that they are always surprised at hearing of a good action and never of a bad one.

John Keats (1795–1821)
British poet.

2 No absolute is going to make the lion lie down with the lamb unless the lamb is inside.

D. H. Lawrence (1885–1930)
British novelist.

3 It is part of human nature to hate the man you have hurt.

Tacitus (c. 55–c. 120 AD)
Roman historian.

HUMILITY

1 It is difficult to be humble. Even if you aim at humility, there is no guarantee that when you have attained the state you will not be proud of the feat.

Bonamy Dobrée (1891–1974)
British scholar and writer.

2 The meek do not inherit the earth unless they are prepared to fight for their meekness.

H. J. Laski (1893–1950)
British political theorist.

3 I too had thoughts once of being an intellectual, but I found it too difficult.

Albert Schweitzer (1875–1965)
French Protestant theologian, philosopher, and physician.
Remark made to an African who refused to perform a menial task on
the grounds that he was an intellectual

HUMOUR

1   The marvellous thing about a joke with a double meaning
is that it can only mean one thing.

Ronnie Barker (1929–)
British comedian.

2   Men will confess to treason, murder, arson, false teeth, or
a wig. How many of them will own up to a lack of
humour?

Frank More Colby (1865–1925)
US editor.

3   It's hard to be funny when you have to be clean.

Mae West (1892–1980)
US actress.

SOME EXAMPLES

4   I do most of my work sitting down; that's where I shine.

Robert Benchley (1889–1945)
US humorist.

5   Dear 338171 (May I call you 338?).

Noël Coward (1899–1973)
British dramatist.
Starting a letter to T. E. Lawrence who had retired from public life to
become Aircraftsman Brown, 338171

6 Please accept my resignation. I don't want to belong to any club that will accept me as a member.

Groucho Marx (Julius Marx; 1895–1977)
US comedian.
Resigning from the Friar's Club in Hollywood

7 Oh, don't worry about Alan…Alan will always land on somebody's feet.

Dorothy Parker (1893–1967)
US writer.
Said of her husband on the day their divorce became final

HUNTING

1 There is a passion for *hunting something* deeply implanted in the human breast.

Charles Dickens (1812–1870)
British novelist.

2 It is very strange, and very melancholy, that the paucity of human pleasures should persuade us ever to call hunting one of them.

Samuel Johnson (1709–84)
British lexicographer.

3 When a man wantonly destroys one of the works of man we call him a vandal. When he destroys one of the works of God we call him a sportsman.

Joseph Wood Krutch (1893–1970)
US essayist.

4 When a man wants to murder a tiger he calls it sport; when a tiger wants to murder him he calls it ferocity.

George Bernard Shaw (1856–1950)
Irish dramatist and critic.

5   The birds seem to consider the muzzle of my gun as their safest position.

Sydney Smith (1771–1845)
English writer and clergyman.

6   It is the sport of kings, the image of war without its guilt, and only five-and-twenty per cent of its danger.

R. S. Surtees (1803–64)
English novelist.

7   The English country gentleman galloping after a fox – the unspeakable in full pursuit of the uneatable.

Oscar Wilde (1854–1900)
Irish-born British dramatist.

HYPOCRISY

1   Man is the only animal that can remain on friendly terms with the victims he intends to eat until he eats them.

Samuel Butler (1835–1902)
British writer.

2   The book written against fame and learning has the author's name on the title-page.

Ralph Waldo Emerson (1803–82)
US poet and essayist.

3   The man who murdered his parents, then pleaded for mercy on the grounds that he was an orphan.

Abraham Lincoln (1809–65)
US statesman.
Defining a hypocrite

4   Hypocrisy is the homage paid by vice to virtue.

Duc de la Rochefoucauld (1613–80)
French writer.

IDEALISM

1   You can't be a true idealist without being a true realist.

Jacques Delors (1925–)
French politician and economist.

2   If a man hasn't discovered something that he would die for, he isn't fit to live.

Martin Luther King (1929–68)
US Black civil-rights leader.

3   An idealist is one who, on noticing that a rose smells better than a cabbage, concludes that it will also make better soup.

H. L. Mencken (1880–1956)
US journalist.

4   A radical is a man with both feet firmly planted in the air.

Franklin D. Roosevelt (1882–1945)
US Democratic president.

IDEAS

1   What was once thought can never be unthought.

Friedrich Dürrenmatt (1921–90)
Swiss writer.

2   The mind, once expanded to the dimensions of larger ideas, never returns to its original size.

Oliver Wendell Holmes (1809–94)
US physician.

3   A stand can be made against invasion by an army; no
stand can be made against invasion by an idea.

Victor Hugo (1802–85)
French writer.

4   An idea isn't responsible for the people who believe in it.

Don Marquis (1878–1937)
US journalist.

5   The human mind treats a new idea in the same way the
body treats a strange protein; it rejects it.

Peter Medawar (1915–87)
British immunologist.

IDLENESS

1   Idleness is only the refuge of weak minds.

Earl of Chesterfield (1694–1773)
English statesman.

2   I like work; it fascinates me. I can sit and look at it for
hours. I love to keep it by me; the idea of getting rid of it
nearly breaks my heart.

Jerome K. Jerome (1859–1927)
British humorist.

IGNORANCE

1   I wish you would read a little poetry sometimes. Your
ignorance cramps my conversation.

Anthony Hope (Sir Anthony Hope Hawkins; 1863–1933)
British novelist.

2 What you don't know would make a great book.

Sydney Smith (1771–1845)
British clergyman and essayist.

3 Ignorance is like a delicate exotic fruit; touch it, and the bloom is gone.

Oscar Wilde (1854–1900)
Irish-born British dramatist.

ILLNESS

1 I reckon being ill as one of the greatest pleasures of life, provided one is not too ill and is not obliged to work till one is better.

Samuel Butler (1835–1902)
British writer.

2 If you start to think about your physical or moral condition, you usually find that you are sick.

J. W. von Goethe (1749–1832)
German poet and dramatist.

3 Everyone who is born holds dual citizenship, in the kingdom of the well and in the kingdom of the sick. Although we all prefer to use only the good passport, sooner or later each of us is obliged, at least for a spell, to identify ourselves as citizens of that other place.

Susan Sontag (1933–)
US novelist and essayist.

IMAGINATION

1 Were it not for imagination, Sir, a man would be as happy in the arms of a chambermaid as of a Duchess.

Samuel Johnson (1709–84)
British lexocographer.

2 Imagination and fiction make up more than three quarters of our real life.

Simone Weil (1909–43)
French philosopher.

IMPERFECTION

1 When you have faults, do not fear to abandon them.

Confucius (K'ung Fu-tzu; 551–479 BC)
Chinese philosopher.

2 We only confess our little faults to persuade people that we have no large ones.

Duc de la Rochefoucauld (1613–80)
French writer.

3 We are none of us infallible – not even the youngest of us.

William Hepworth Thompson (1810–86)
British academic.
Referring to G. W. Balfour, who was a junior fellow of Trinity College at the time

INATTENTION

1 That should assure us of at least forty-five minutes of undisturbed privacy.

Dorothy Parker (1893–1967)
US writer.
Pressing a button marked NURSE during a stay in hospital

2 I murdered my grandmother this morning.

Franklin D. Roosevelt (1882–1945)
US Democratic president.
His habitual greeting to any guest at the White House he suspected of
paying no attention to what he said

INDECISION

1 I must have a prodigious quantity of mind; it takes me as
much as a week, sometimes, to make it up.

Mark Twain (Samuel Langhorne Clemens; 1835–1910)
US writer.

INDISPENSABILITY

1 She was one of those indispensables of whom one makes
the discovery, when they are gone, that one can get on
quite as well without them.

Aldous Huxley (1894–1964)
British novelist.

INFERIORITY

1 No one can make you feel inferior without your consent.

Eleanor Roosevelt (1884–1962)
US writer and lecturer.

INFLUENCE

1 He who influences the thought of his times, influences all

the times that follow. He has made his impress on eternity.

Hypatia (c. 370–415)
Egyptian Neoplatonist philosopher and mathematician.

2   The proper time to influence the character of a child is about a hundred years before he is born.

Dean Inge (1860–1954)
British churchman.

3   Practical men, who believe themselves to be quite exempt from any intellectual influences, are usually the slaves of some defunct economist.

John Maynard Keynes (1883–1946)
British economist.

INGRATITUDE

1   Our gratitude to most benefactors is the same as our feeling for dentists who have pulled our teeth. We acknowledge the good they have done and the evil from which they have delivered us, but we remember the pain they occasioned and do not love them very much.

Nicolas Chamfort (1741–94)
French writer.

INJUSTICE

1   When one has been threatened with a great injustice, one accepts a smaller as a favour.

Jane Welsh Carlyle (1801–66)
The wife of Thomas Carlyle.

2 I feel as a horse must feel when the beautiful cup is given to the jockey.

Edgar Degas (1934–17)
French artist.
On seeing one of his pictures sold at auction

INSENSITIVITY

1 One would have to have a heart of stone to read the death of Little Nell without laughing.

Oscar Wilde (1854–1900)
Irish-born British dramatist.
Lecturing upon Dickens

INSINCERITY

1 Experience teaches you that the man who looks you straight in the eye, particularly if he adds a firm handshake, is hiding something.

Clifton Fadiman (1904–)
US writer.

INSULTS

1 She looked as though butter wouldn't melt in her mouth – or anywhere else.

Elsa Lanchester (1902–86)
British-born US actress.
Referring to Maureen O'Hara

2 Like a cushion, he always bore the impress of the last man who sat on him.

David Lloyd George (1863–1945)
British Liberal statesman.
Referring to Lord Derby

3 When they circumcised Herbert Samuel they threw away the wrong bit.

David Lloyd George

4 A triumph of the embalmer's art.

Gore Vidal (1925–)
US novelist.
Referring to Ronald Reagan

5 A typical triumph of modern science to find the only part of Randolph that was not malignant and remove it.

Evelyn Waugh (1903–66)
British novelist.
Remarking upon the news that Randolph Churchill had had a noncancerous lung removed

6 You have Van Gogh's ear for music.

Billy Wilder (Samuel Wilder; 1906–)
Austrian-born US film director.
Said to Cliff Osmond

7 I have always said about Tony that he immatures with age.

Harold Wilson (1916–95)
British politician and prime minister.
Referring to Anthony Wedgwood Benn

INTELLECT

1 An intellectual is a man who doesn't know how to park a bike.

Spiro Agnew (1918–96)
US politician.

2 Intellectuals are people who believe that ideas are of more importance than values. That is to say, their own ideas and other people's values.

Gerald Brenan (Edward Fitzgerald Brenan; 1894–1987)
British writer.

3 Intelligence is almost useless to the person whose only quality it is.

Alexis Carrel (1873–1944)
French surgeon.

4 The highest intellects, like the tops of mountains, are the first to catch and to reflect the dawn.

Lord Macaulay (1800–59)
British historian.

5 The higher the voice the smaller the intellect.

Ernest Newman (1868–1959)
British music critic.

6 What is a highbrow? It is a man who has found something more interesting than women.

Edgar Wallace (1875–1932)
British thriller writer.

7 All the unhappy marriages come from the husbands having brains. What good are brains to a man? They only unsettle him.

P. G. Wodehouse (1881–1975)
British humorous novelist.

IRELAND

1 All races have produced notable economists, with the

exception of the Irish who doubtless can protest their devotion to higher arts.

John Kenneth Galbraith (1908–)
US economist.

2   Worth seeing? yes; but not worth going to see.

Samuel Johnson (1709–84)
British lexicographer.
Referring to the Giant's Causeway

3   The Irish are a fair people; – they never speak well of one another.

Samuel Johnson

4   The problem with Ireland is that it's a country full of genius, but with absolutely no talent.

Hugh Leonard (1926–)
Irish dramatist.
Said during an interview

5   It is a city where you can see a sparrow fall to the ground, and God watching it.

Conor Cruise O'Brien (1917–)
Irish diplomat and writer.
Referring to Dublin

6   The English should give Ireland home rule – and reserve the motion picture rights.

Will Rogers (1879–1935)
US actor and humorist.

7   A disease in the family that is never mentioned.

William Trevor (W. T. Cox; 1928–)
Irish writer.
Referring to the Troubles in Northern Ireland

JEALOUSY

1   The others were only my wives. But you, my dear, will be my widow.

Sacha Guitry (1885–1957)
French actor and dramatist.
Allaying his fifth wife's jealousy of his previous wives

JEWS

1   The gentleman will please remember that when his half-civilized ancestors were hunting the wild boar in Silesia, mine were princes of the earth.

Judah Philip Benjamin (1811–84)
US politician.
Replying to a senator of Germanic origin who had made an antisemitic remark

2   I believe that the Jews have made a contribution to the human condition out of all proportion to their numbers: I believe them to be an immense people. Not only have they supplied the world with two leaders of the stature of Jesus Christ and Karl Marx, but they have even indulged in the luxury of following neither one nor the other.

Peter Ustinov (1921–)
British actor.

JUDGMENT

1   Consider what you think justice requires, and decide accordingly. But never give your reasons; for your judgement will probably be right, but your reasons will certainly be wrong.

Lord Mansfield (1705–93)
British judge and politician.
Advice given to a new colonial governor

2   Everyone complains of his memory, but no one complains of his judgement.

Duc de la Rochefoucauld (1613–80)
French writer.

JUSTICE

1   I'm arm'd with more than complete steel –
The justice of my quarrel.

Christopher Marlowe (1564–93)
English dramatist.
Play also attributed to others

2   In England, Justice is open to all, like the Ritz hotel.

James Mathew (1830–1908)
British judge.
Also attrib. to Lord Darling

3   Under a government which imprisons any unjustly, the true place for a just man is also a prison.

Henry David Thoreau (1817–62)
US writer.

KINDNESS

1   I love thee for a heart that's kind –
Not for the knowledge in thy mind.

W. H. Davies (1871–1940)
British poet.

2   So many gods, so many creeds,

So many paths that wind and wind,
While just the art of being kind
Is all the sad world needs.

Ella Wheeler Wilcox (1850–1919)
US poet.

KNOWLEDGE

1   The fox knows many things – the hedgehog one *big* one.

   Archilochus (c. 680–c. 640 BC)
   Greek poet.

2   It is the province of knowledge to speak and it is the privilege of wisdom to listen.

   Oliver Wendell Holmes (1809–94)
   US writer.

3   All knowledge is of itself of some value. There is nothing so minute or inconsiderable, that I would not rather know it than not.

   Samuel Johnson (1709–84)
   British lexicographer.

4   Knowledge is of two kinds. We know a subject ourselves, or we know where we can find information upon it.

   Samuel Johnson

5   Learning is a treasure which accompanies its owner everywhere.

   Proverb

LAUGHTER

1 The most wasted of all days is that on which one has not laughed.

Nicolas Chamfort (1741–94)
French writer.

LAZINESS

1 You have to be efficient if you're going to be lazy.

Shirley Conran (1932–)
British designer and writer.

2 I get my exercise acting as a pallbearer to my friends who exercise.

Chauncey Depew (1834–1928)
US politician.

3 For one person who dreams of making fifty thousands pounds, a hundred people dream of being left fifty thousand pounds.

A. A. Milne (1882–1956)
British writer.

LEADERSHIP

1 'She still seems to me in her own way a person born to command,' said Luce…
'I wonder if anyone is born to obey,' said Isabel.
'That may be why people command rather

badly, that they have no suitable material to
work on.'

Ivy Compton-Burnett (1892–1969)
British novelist.

2   Let me pass, I have to follow them, I am their leader.

Alexandre Auguste Ledru-Rollin (1807–74)
French lawyer and politician.
Trying to force his way through a mob during the
Revolution of 1848, of which he was one of the chief instigators. A
similar remark is attributed to Bonar Law.

LEAVING

1   I will undoubtedly have to seek what is happily known as
gainful employment, which I am glad to say does not
describe holding public office.

Dean Acheson (1893–1971)
US lawyer and statesman.

2   It is amazing how nice people are to you when they know
you are going away.

Michael Arlen (1895–1956)
British novelist.

3   It is never any good dwelling on goodbyes. It is not the
being together that it prolongs, it is the parting.

Elizabeth Bibesco (1897–1945)
British writer.

4   Absence is to love what wind is to fire; it extinguishes the
small, it inflames the great.

Bussy-Rabutin (Roger de Rabutin, Comte de Bussy; 1618–93)
French soldier and writer.

5   All farewells should be sudden.

Lord Byron (1788–1824)
British poet.

6   Retirement from the concert world is like giving up
smoking. You have got to finish completely.

Beniamino Gigli (1890–1957)
Italian tenor.

7   He had said he had known many kicked down stairs, but
he never knew any kicked up stairs before.

Lord Halifax (1633–95)
English statesman.

8   Have you ever been out for a late autumn walk in the
closing part of the afternoon, and suddenly looked up to
realize that the leaves have practically all gone? And the
sun has set and the day gone before you knew it – and
with that a cold wind blows across the landscape? That's
retirement.

Stephen Leacock (1869–1944)
English-born Canadian economist and humorist.

9   There comes a time in every man's life when he must
make way for an older man.

Reginald Maudling (1917–77)
British politician.
Remark made on being replaced in the shadow cabinet by John
Davies, his elder by four years

10   Eating's going to be a whole new ball game. I may even
have to buy a new pair of trousers.

Lester Piggot (1935–)
British champion jockey.
On his retirement

11 Fear no more the heat o' the sun,
Nor the furious winter's rages;
Thou thy worldly task hast done,
Home art gone and ta'en thy wages.

William Shakespeare (1564–1616)
English dramatist.

12 Good night, good night! Parting is such
sweet sorrow
That I shall say good night till it be morrow.

William Shakespeare

13 When a man retires and time is no longer a matter of
urgent importance, his colleagues generally present him
with a clock.

R. C. Sherriff (1896–1975)
British author.

LEISURE

1 We are closer to the ants than to the butterflies. Very few
people can endure much leisure.

Gerald Brenan (Edward Fitzgerald Brenan; 1894–1987)
British writer.

2 It is necessary to be slightly underemployed if you want
to do something significant.

James Dewey Watson (1928–)
US biochemist.

LIFE

1 Life is rather like a tin of sardines – we're all of us looking
for the key.

Alan Bennett (1934–)
British playwright.

2 Life is a tragedy when seen in close-up, but a comedy in long-shot.

Charlie Chaplin (Sir Charles Spencer C.; 1889–1977)
British film actor.

3 Life is a maze in which we take the wrong turning before we have learnt to walk.

Cyril Connolly (1903–74)
British journalist.

4 Life is like a sewer. What you get out of it depends on what you put into it.

Tom Lehrer (1928–)
US university teacher and songwriter.

5 Life is what happens to you while you're busy making other plans.

John Lennon (1940–80)
British rock musician.

LOGIC

1 'Contrariwise,' continued Tweedledee, 'if it was so, it might be; and if it were so, it would be; but as it isn't, it ain't. That's logic.'

Lewis Carroll (Charles Lutwidge Dodgson; 1832–98)
British writer.

2 You can only find truth with logic if you have already found truth without it.

G. K. Chesterton (1874–1936)
British writer.

LONDON

1 I think the full tide of human existence is at Charing-Cross.

Samuel Johnson (1709–84)
British lexicographer.

2 When a man is tired of London, he is tired of life; for there is in London all that life can afford.

Samuel Johnson

3 Crossing Piccadilly Circus.

Joseph Thomson (1858–95)
Scottish explorer.
His reply when asked by J. M. Barrie what was the most hazardous part of his expedition to Africa

LOVE

1 Love is, above all, the gift of oneself.

Jean Anouilh (1910–87)
French dramatist.

2 He was my North, my South, my East and West,
My working week and my Sunday rest,
My noon, my midnight, my talk, my song;
I thought that love would last for ever: I was wrong.

W. H. Auden (1907–73)
British poet.

3 Many a man has fallen in love with a girl in a light so dim he would not have chosen a suit by it.

Maurice Chevalier (1888–1972)
French singer and actor.

4   We don't believe in rheumatism and true love until after
the first attack.

Marie Ebner von Eschenbach (1830–1916)
Austrian writer.

5   When one loves somebody everything is clear – where to
go, what to do – it all takes care of itself and one doesn't
have to ask anybody about anything.

Maxim Gorky (Aleksei Maksimovich Peshkov; 1868–1936)
Russian writer.

6   Love's like the measles – all the worse when it comes late
in life.

Douglas William Jerrold (1803–57)
British dramatist.

7   Love is the delusion that one woman differs from another.

H. L. Mencken (1880–1956)
US journalist.

8   Love does not consist in gazing at each other but in
looking together in the same direction.

Antoine de Saint-Exupéry (1900–44)
French novelist and aviator.

9   True love's the gift which God has given
To man alone beneath the heaven.

Walter Scott (1771–1832)
Scottish novelist.

10   Love conquers all things except poverty and toothache.

Mae West (1892–1980)
US actress.

LOYALTY

1   A man who will steal *for* me will steal *from* me.

Theodore Roosevelt (1858–1919)
US Republican president.
Firing a cowboy who had applied Roosevelt's brand to a steer
belonging to a neighbouring ranch.

2   If this man is not faithful to his God, how can he be
faithful to me, a mere man?

Theodoric (c. 445–526)
King of the Ostrogoths.
Explaining why he had had a trusted minister, who had said he would
adopt his master's religion, beheaded.

LYING

1   A lie can be half-way round the world before the truth has
got its boots on.

James Callaghan (1912–)
British politician and prime minister.

2   A lie is an abomination unto the Lord and a very present
help in trouble.

Adlai Stevenson (1900–65)
US statesman.

MADNESS

1   The madman is not the man who has lost his reason. The
madman is the man who has lost everything except his
reason.

G. K. Chesterton (1874–1936)
British writer.

2 Every one is more or less mad on one point.

Rudyard Kipling (1865–1936)
Indian-born British writer.

3 Insanity in individuals is something rare – but in groups, parties, nations, and epochs it is the rule.

Friedrich Nietzsche (1844–1900)
German philosopher.

MANNERS

1 On the Continent people have good food; in England people have good table manners.

George Mikes (1912–87)
Hungarian-born British writer.

2 Good breeding consists in concealing how much we think of ourselves and how little we think of other persons.

Mark Twain (Samuel Langhorne Clemens; 1835–1910)
US writer.

MARRIAGE

1 Bigamy is having one wife too many. Monogamy is the same thing.

Anonymous

2 *Marriage,* n. The state or condition of a community consisting of a master, a mistress and two slaves, making in all two.

Ambrose Bierce (1842–?1914)
US writer and journalist.

3 Marriage has many pains, but celibacy has no pleasures.

Samuel Johnson (1709–84)
British lexicographer.

4 Marrying a man is like buying something you've been admiring in a shop window. You may love it when you get home, but it doesn't always go with everything else in the house.

Jean Kerr (1923–)
US dramatist.

5 The men that women marry,
And why they marry them, will always be
A marvel and a mystery to the world.

Henry Wadsworth Longfellow (1807–82)
US poet.

6 Marriage is a wonderful institution, but who wants to live in an institution?

Groucho Marx (Julius Marx; 1895–1977)
US comedian.

7 One doesn't have to get anywhere in a marriage. It's not a public conveyance.

Iris Murdoch (1919–99)
Irish-born British novelist.

8 A loving wife will do anything for her husband except stop criticising and trying to improve him.

J. B. Priestley (1894–1984)
British novelist.

9 When you're bored with yourself, marry and be bored with someone else.

David Pryce-Jones (1936–)
British author and critic.

10 A married couple are well suited when both partners usually feel the need for a quarrel at the same time.

Jean Rostand (1894–1977)
French biologist and writer.

11 Never feel remorse for what you have thought about your wife; she has thought much worse things about you.

Jean Rostand

12 It takes two to make a marriage a success and only one a failure.

Herbert Samuel (1870–1963)
British Liberal statesman.

13 My definition of marriage:….it resembles a pair of shears, so joined that they cannot be separated; often moving in opposite directions, yet always punishing anyone who comes between them.

Sydney Smith (1771–1845)
British clergyman and essayist.

14 A man should not insult his wife publicly, at parties. He should insult her in the privacy of the home.

James Thurber (1894–1961)
US humorist.

15 Twenty years of romance makes a woman look like a ruin; but twenty years of marriage make her something like a public building.

Oscar Wilde (1854–1900)
Irish-born British dramatist.

16 The best part of married life is the fights. The rest is merely so-so.

Thornton Wilder (1897–1975)
US novelist and dramatist.

MATERIALISM

1 In a consumer society there are inevitably two kinds of slaves: the prisoners of addiction and the prisoners of envy.

Ivan Illich (1926–)
US sociologist.

MEDIA

1 A medium, so called because it is neither rare nor well done.

Ernie Kovacs (1919–62)
US entertainer.
Referring to television. Attrib.

2 I'm with you on the free press. It's the newspapers I can't stand.

Tom Stoppard (1937–)
Czech-born British dramatist.

3 Freedom of the press in Britain is freedom to print such of the proprietor's prejudices as the advertisers don't object to.

Hannan Swaffer (1879–1962)
British journalist.
Attrib.

MEDICINE

1   I am dying with the help of too many physicians.

Alexander the Great (356–323 BC)
King of Macedon.

2   One of the most difficult things to contend with in a hospital is the assumption on the part of the staff that because you have lost your gall bladder you have also lost your mind.

Jean Kerr (1923–)
US dramatist.

MEMORY

1   I never forget a face, but I'll make an exception in your case.

Groucho Marx (Julius Marx; 1895–1977)
US comedian.

2   To expect a man to retain everything that he has ever read is like expecting him to carry about in his body everything that he has ever eaten.

Arthur Schopenhauer (1788–1860)
German philosopher.

MEN

1   I base everything on the idea that all men are basically just seven years old.

Joan Collins (1933–)
British actress.

2   The male ego with few exceptions is elephantine to start with.

Bette Davis (Ruth Elizabeth D.; 1908–89)
US actress.

3   I never hated a man enough to give him diamonds back.

Zsa Zsa Gabor (1919–)
Hungarian-born US film star.

4   Sometimes I think if there was a third sex men wouldn't get so much as a glance from me.

Amanda Vail (Warren Miller; 1921–66)
US writer.

5   A man in the house is worth two in the street.

Mae West (1892–1980)
US actress.

MEN AND WOMEN

1   The reason that husbands and wives do not understand each other is because they belong to different sexes.

Dorothy Dix (Elizabeth Meriwether Gilmer; 1861–1951)
US journalist and writer.

2   Men don't understand anything about women and women understand nothing about men. And it's better that way.

Vittorio Gassman (1922–)
Italian actor.

3   Where young boys plan for what they will achieve and attain, young girls plan for whom they will achieve and attain.

Charlotte Perkins Gilman (1860–1935)
US writer.

4 Fighting is essentially a masculine idea; a woman's
weapon is her tongue.

Hermione Gingold (1897–1987)
British actress.

5 Strange difference of sex, that time and circumstance,
which enlarge the views of most men, narrows the views
of women almost invariably.

Thomas Hardy (1840–1928)
British novelist.

6 Man has his will, – but woman has her way.

Oliver Wendell Holmes (1809–94)
US writer.

7 Women want mediocre men, and men are working to be
as mediocre as possible.

Margaret Mead (1901–78)
US anthropologist.

8 A woman needs a man like a fish needs a bicycle.

Proverb

9 I do, and I also wash and iron them.

Denis Thatcher (1915–)
British businessman, husband of Margaret Thatcher.
Replying to the question "Who wears the pants in this house?"

10 When a man confronts catastrophe on the road, he looks
in his purse – but a woman looks in her mirror.

Margaret Turnbull (fl. 1920s–1942)
US writer.

11   Why are women…so much more interesting to men than men are to women?

Virginia Woolf (1882–1941)
British novelist.

MERIT

1   I guess this is the week I earn my salary.

John Fitzgerald Kennedy (1917–63)
US statesman.
Comment made during the Cuban missile crisis

2   I wasn't lucky. I deserved it.

Margaret Thatcher (1925–)
British politician and prime minister.
Said after receiving school prize, aged nine. Attrib.

MISFORTUNE

1   Calamities are of two kinds. Misfortune to ourselves and good fortune to others.

Ambrose Bierce (1842–?1914)
US writer and journalist.

2   We are all strong enough to bear the misfortunes of others.

Duc de la Rochefoucauld (1613–80)
French writer.

MISTAKES

1   Better send them a Papal Bull.

Lord Curzon (1859–1925)
British politician.
Written in the margin of a Foreign Office document. The phrase 'the monks of Mount Athos were violating their vows' had been misprinted as '...violating their cows'.

2   Yes, once – many, many years ago. I thought I had made a wrong decision. Of course, it turned out that I had been right all along. But I was wrong to have *thought* that I was wrong.

John Foster Dulles (1888–1959)
US politician.
On being asked whether he had ever been wrong

3   The physician can bury his mistakes, but the architect can only advise his clients to plant vines.

Frank Lloyd Wright (1869–1959)
US architect.

4   The man who makes no mistakes does not usually make anything.

Edward John Phelps (1822–1900)
US lawyer and diplomat.

5   The follies which a man regrets the most in his life, are those which he didn't commit when he had the opportunity.

Helen Rowland (1876–1950)
US writer.

6   What time is the next swan?

Leo Slezak (1873–1946)
Czechoslovakian-born tenor.
When the mechanical swan left the stage without him during a performance of *Lohengrin*

MISTRUST

1 The lion and the calf shall lie down together but the calf won't get much sleep.

Woody Allen (Allen Stewart Konigsberg; 1935–)
US film actor.

MONEY

1 A rich man is one who isn't afraid to ask the salesman to show him something cheaper.

Anonymous

2 A man who has a million dollars is as well off as if he were rich.

John Jacob Astor (1763–1848)
US millionaire.

3 Money is like muck, not good except it be spread.

Francis Bacon (1561–1626)
English philosopher.
See also MURCHISON

4 Money, it turned out, was exactly like sex, you thought of nothing else if you didn't have it and thought of other things if you did.

James Baldwin (1924–87)
US writer.

5 If you can actually count your money you are not really a rich man.

J. Paul Getty (1892–1976)
US oil magnate.

6 There are few ways in which a man can be more innocently employed than in getting money.

Samuel Johnson (1709–84)
British lexicographer.

7 You don't seem to realize that a poor person who is unhappy is in a better position than a rich person who is unhappy. Because the poor person has hope. He thinks money would help.

Jean Kerr (1923–)
US dramatist.

8 What's a thousand dollars? Mere chicken feed. A poultry matter.

Groucho Marx (Julius Marx; 1895–1977)
US comedian.

9 Money can't buy friends, but you can get a better class of enemy.

Spike Milligan (1918–)
British comic actor and author.

10 Money is like manure. If you spread it around it does a lot of good. But if you pile it up in one place it stinks like hell.

Clint Murchison Jnr (1895–1969)
US industrialist.

11 God shows his contempt for wealth by the kind of person he selects to receive it.

Austin O'Malley (1858–1932)
US writer.

12 Money doesn't make you happy. I now have $50 million but I was just as happy when I had $48 million.

Arnold Schwarzenegger (1947–)
US film actor.

13 The trouble, Mr Goldwyn is that you are only interested in art and I am only interested in money.

George Bernard Shaw (1856–1950)
Irish dramatist and critic.
Turning down Goldwyn's offer to buy the screen rights of his plays

14 It is the wretchedness of being rich that you have to live with rich people.

Logan Pearsall Smith (1865–1946)
US writer.

15 That's right. 'Taint yours, and 'taint mine.

Mark Twain (Samuel Langhorne Clemens; 1835–1910)
US writer.
Agreeing with a friend's comment that the money of a particular rich industrialist was 'tainted'.

16 There's something about a crowd like that that brings a lump to my wallet.

Eli Wallach (1915–)
US actor.
Remarking upon the long line of people at the box office before one of his performances

17 You can be young without money but you can't be old without it.

Tennessee Williams (1911–83)
US dramatist.

MORALITY

1 Give me chastity and continence, but not yet.

St Augustine of Hippo (354–430)
Bishop of Hippo.

2 No morality can be founded on authority, even if the authority were divine.

A. J. Ayer (1910–89)
British philosopher.

3 Morality is only expediency in a long white dress.

Quentin Crisp (c. 1910–)
British model, publicist, and writer.

4 What is moral is what you feel good after, and what is immoral is what you feel bad after.

Ernest Hemingway (1899–1961)
US novelist.

5 The Puritan hated bear-baiting, not because it gave pain to the bear, but because it gave pleasure to the spectators.

Lord Macaulay (1800–59)
British historian.

6 Puritanism – The haunting fear that someone, somewhere, may be happy.

H. L. Mencken (1880–1956)
US journalist.

7 Morality consists in suspecting other people of not being legally married.

George Bernard Shaw (1856–1950)
Irish dramatist and critic.

8 The so-called new morality is too often the old immorality condoned.

Lord Shawcross (1902–)
British Labour politician and lawyer.

9 Moral indignation is in most cases 2 percent moral, 48 percent indignation and 50 percent envy.

Vittorio De Sica (1901–74)
Italian film director.

MORTALITY

1 They are not long, the days of wine and roses.

Ernest Dowson (1867–1900)
British lyric poet.

2 All humane things are subject to decay,
And, when Fate summons, Monarchs must obey.

John Dryden (1631–1700)
British poet and dramatist.

3 A little rule, a little sway,
A sunbeam in a winter's day,
Is all the proud and mighty have
Between the cradle and the grave.

John Dyer (1700–58)
British poet.

4 Is life a boon?
If so, it must befall
That Death, whene'er he call,
Must call too soon.

W. S. Gilbert (1836–1911)
British dramatist.
The lines are written on Arthur Sullivan's memorial

5 The boast of heraldry, the pomp of pow'r,
And all that beauty, all that wealth e'er gave,
Awaits alike th' inevitable hour,
The paths of glory lead but to the grave.

Thomas Gray (1716–71)
British poet.

6 I expect to pass through this world but once; any good
thing therefore that I can do, or any kindness that I can
show to any fellow-creature, let me do it now; let me not
defer or neglect it, for I shall not pass this way again.

Stephen Grellet (1773–1855)
French-born US missionary.
Attrib.

7 I am moved to pity, when I think of the brevity of human
life, seeing that of all this host of men not one will still be
alive in a hundred years' time.

Xerxes (d. 465 BC)
King of Persia.
On surveying his army

MUSIC

1 The music teacher came twice each week to bridge the
awful gap between Dorothy and Chopin.

George Ade (1866–1944)
US dramatist and humorist.

2 Brass bands are all very well in their place – outdoors and
several miles away.

Thomas Beecham (1879–1961)
British conductor.

3 The English may not like music – but they absolutely love the noise it makes.

Thomas Beecham

4 The sound of the harpsichord resembles that of a bird-cage played with toasting-forks.

Thomas Beecham

5 People are wrong when they say the opera isn't what it used to be. It is what it used to be. That's what's wrong with it.

Noël Coward (1899–1973)
British dramatist.

6 Composing a piece of music is very feminine. It is sensitive, emotional, contemplative. By comparison, doing housework is positively masculine.

Barbara Kolb (1939–)
US composer.

7 To be played with both hands in the pocket.

Erik Satie (1866–1925)
French composer.
Direction on one of his piano pieces

8 After I die, I shall return to earth as a gatekeeper of a bordello and I won't let any of you – not a one of you – enter!

Arturo Toscanini (1867–1957)
Italian conductor.
Rebuking an incompetent orchestra

NAKEDNESS

1 No, you see there are portions of the human anatomy which would keep swinging after the music had finished.

Robert Helpmann (1909–86)
Australian ballet dancer, choreographer, and actor.
When asked whether the fashion for stage nudity would ever spread to the ballet

2 JOURNALIST. Didn't you have anything on?
M. M. I had the radio on.

Marilyn Monroe (Norma-Jean Baker; 1926–62)
US film star.

NATURE

1 Though you drive away Nature with a pitchfork she always returns.

Horace (Quintus Horatius Flaccus; 65 BC–8 BC)
Roman poet.

2 In nature there are neither rewards nor punishments – there are consequences.

Robert G. Ingersoll (1833–99)
US lawyer and agnostic.

3 Nature is usually wrong.

James Whistler (1834–1903)
US painter.

NOBILITY

1 His life was gentle, and the elements
So mixed in him that Nature might stand up
And say to all the world, 'This was a man!'

William Shakespeare (1564–1616)
English dramatist.

2 There is
One great society alone on earth:
The noble living and the noble dead.

William Wordsworth (1770–1850)
British poet.

NONCOMMITMENT

1 We know what happens to people who stay in the middle of the road. They get run over.

Aneurin Bevan (1897–1960)
British Labour politician.

2 The Right Hon. gentleman has sat so long on the fence that the iron has entered his soul.

David Lloyd George (1863–1945)
British Liberal statesman.
Referring to Sir John Simon

3 The man who sees both sides of a question is a man who sees absolutely nothing at all.

Oscar Wilde (1854–1900)
Irish-born British dramatist.

NOSTALGIA

1 They spend their time mostly looking forward to the past.

John Osborne (1929–94)
British dramatist.

2 Sweet childish days that were as long
As twenty days are now.

William Wordsworth (1770–1850)
British poet.

OBESITY

1 Outside every fat man there is an even fatter man trying to close in.

Kingsley Amis (1922–95)
British novelist.
See also ORWELL

2 Just the other day in the Underground I enjoyed the pleasure of offering my seat to three ladies.

G. K. Chesterton (1874–1936)
British writer.
Suggesting that fatness has its consolations

3 I'm fat, but I'm thin inside. Has it ever struck you that there's a thin man inside every fat man, just as they say there's a statue inside every block of stone?

George Orwell (Eric Blair; 1903–50)
See also AMIS
British novelist.

4 My advice if you insist on slimming: Eat as much as you like – just don't swallow it.

Harry Secombe (1921–)
Welsh singer, actor, and comedian.

OBITUARIES

1 With the newspaper strike on I wouldn't consider it.

Bette Davis (Ruth Elizabeth Davis; 1908–89)
US film star.
When told that a rumour was spreading that she had died

2 I've just read that I am dead. Don't forget to delete me from your list of subscribers.

Rudyard Kipling (1865–1936)
Indian-born British writer.
Writing to a magazine that had mistakenly published an announcement of his death

3 Reports of my death are greatly exaggerated.

Mark Twain (Samuel Langhorne Clemens; 1835–1910)
US writer.
On learning that his obituary had been published

OCCUPATIONS

ACTORS

1 For an actress to be a success she must have the face of Venus, the brains of Minerva, the grace of Terpsichore, the memory of Macaulay, the figure of Juno, and the hide of a rhinoceros.

Ethel Barrymore (1897–1959)
US actress.

2 An actor is something less than a man, while an actress is something more than a woman.

Richard Burton (1925–84)
British actor.

3 When an actor has money he doesn't send letters, he sends telegrams.

Anton Chekhov (1860–1904)
Russian dramatist.

4 Show me a great actor and I'll show you a lousy husband. Show me a great actress, and you've seen the devil.

W. C. Fields (1880–1946)
US actor.

5 Have patience with the jealousies and petulance of actors, for their hour is their eternity.

Richard Garnett (1835–1906)
British writer.

6 Acting is the most minor of gifts. After all, Shirley Temple could do it when she was four.

Katharine Hepburn (1907–)
US actress.

7 The art of acting is not to act. Once you show them more, what you show them in fact, is bad acting.

Anthony Hopkins (1937–)
British actor.

8 Actresses will happen in the best regulated families.

Oliver Herford (1863–1935)
British-born US humorist.

9 Some of the greatest love affairs I've known involved one actor – unassisted.

Wilson Mizner (1876–1933)
US writer and wit.

10 Scratch an actor and you'll find an actress.

Dorothy Parker (1893–1967)
US writer.

11 A character actor is one who cannot act and therefore makes an elaborate study of disguise and stage tricks by which acting can be grotesquely simulated.

George Bernard Shaw (1856–1950)
Irish dramatist and critic.

12 An actor is never so great as when he reminds you of an animal – falling like a cat, lying like a dog, moving like a fox.

François Truffaut (1932–84)
French film director.

13 Every actor in his heart believes everything bad that's printed about him.

Orson Welles (1915–85)
US film director.

14 You can pick out actors by the glazed look that comes into their eyes when the conversation wanders away from themselves.

Michael Wilding (1912–79)
British actor.

ARTISTS

15 Modern art is what happens when painters stop looking

at girls and persuade themselves that they have a better
idea.

John Ciardi (1916–86)
US poet and critic.

16 There has never been a boy painter, nor can there be. The
art requires a long apprenticeship, being *mechanical* as
well as intellectual.

John Constable (1776–1837)
British landscape painter.

17 I do not paint a portrait to look like the subject, rather
does the person grow to look like his portrait.

Salvador Dali (1904–89)
Spanish painter.

18 It is very good advice to believe only what an artist does,
rather than what he says about his work.

David Hockney (1937–)
British painter.

19 There is nothing more difficult for a truly creative painter
than to paint a rose, because before he can do so he has
first to forget all the roses that were ever painted.

Henri Matisse (1869–1954)
French painter and sculptor.

20 Artists, as a rule, do not live in the purple; they live
mainly in the red.

Lord Pearce (1901–85)
British judge.

21 There are painters who transform the sun into a yellow spot, but there are others who, thanks to their art and intelligence, transform a yellow spot into the sun.

Pablo Picasso (1881–1973)
Spanish painter.

22 An artist must know how to convince others of the truth of his lies.

Pablo Picasso

23 The artist who always paints the same scene pleases the public for the sole reason that it recognises him with ease and thinks itself a connoisseur.

Alfred Stevens (1818–75)
British artist.

24 An artist is someone who produces things that people don't need to have but that he – for *some* reason – thinks it would be a good idea to give them.

Andy Warhol (Andrew Warhola; 1926–87)
US artist.

AUTHORS

25 When I want to read a novel I write one.

Benjamin Disraeli (1804–81)
British statesman.

26 The author who speaks about his own books is almost as bad as a mother who talks about her own children.

Benjamin Disraeli

27 The best way to become a successful writer is to read good writing, remember it, and then forget where you remember it from.

Gene Fowler (1890–1960)
US author.

28 No author is a man of genius to his publisher.

Heinrich Heine (1797–1856)
German poet and writer.

29 Abuse is often of service. There is nothing so dangerous to an author as silence.

Samuel Johnson (1709–84)
British lexicographer.

30 No man but a blockhead ever wrote except for money.

Samuel Johnson

31 Authors are easy to get on with – if you're fond of children.

Michael Joseph (1897–1958)
British publisher.

32 No regime has ever loved great writers, only minor ones.

Alexander Solzhenitsyn (1918–)
Russian novelist.

33 Most writers regard truth as their most valuable possession, and therefore are most economical in its use.

Mark Twain (Samuel Langhorne Clemens; 1835–1910)
US writer.

BOOKSELLERS

34 Gentlemen, you must not mistake me. I admit that he is the sworn foe of our nation, and, if you will, of the whole

human race. But, gentlemen, we must be just to our
enemy. We must not forget that he once shot a bookseller.

Thomas Campbell (1777–1844)
British poet.
Excusing himself in proposing a toast to Napoleon at a literary dinner

CLERGY

35   It is no accident that the symbol of a bishop is a crook,
and the sign of an archbishop is a double-cross.

Dom Gregory Dix (1901–52)
British monk.

36   How can a bishop marry? How can he flirt? The most he
can say is, 'I will see you in the vestry after service.'

Sydney Smith (1771–1845)
British clergyman and essayist.

37   I never saw, heard, nor read, that the clergy were beloved
in any nation where Christianity was the religion of the
country. Nothing can render them popular but some
degree of persecution.

Jonathan Swift (1667–1745)
Irish-born Anglican priest and writer.

COOKS

38   We may live without friends; we may live without books;
But civilized man cannot live without cooks.

Owen Meredith (Robert Bulmer-Lytton, 1st Earl of Lytton; 1831–91)
British statesman and poet.

39   The only good thing about him is his cook. The world
visits his dinners, not him.

Molière (Jean Baptiste Poquelin; 1622–73)
French dramatist.

40 The cook was a good cook, as cooks go; and as cooks go, she went.

Saki (Hector Hugh Munro; 1870–1916)
British writer.

CRITICS

41 Critics!… Those cut-throat bandits in the paths of fame.

Robert Burns (1759–96)
Scottish poet.

42 I always get the heaves in the presence of critics.

Gene Fowler (1890–1960)
US author.

43 Asking a working writer what he thinks about critics is like asking a lamp-post how it feels about dogs.

Christopher Hampton (1946–)
British writer and dramatist.

44 A drama critic is a person who surprises the playwright by informing him what he meant.

Wilson Mizner (1876–1933)
US writer and wit.

45 A critic is a legless man who teaches running.

Channing Pollock

46 A critic is a man who knows the way but can't drive the car.

Kenneth Tynan (1927–80)
British theatre critic.

47 Has anybody ever seen a dramatic critic in the daytime?
Of course not. They come out after dark, up to no good.

P. G. Wodehouse (1881–1975)
British humorous novelist.

DOCTORS

48 The threat of a neglected cold is for doctors what the
threat of purgatory is for priests – a gold mine.

Sébastien Chamfort

49 God heals and the doctor takes the fee.

Benjamin Franklin (1706–90)
US scientist and statesman.

50 The doctor found, when she was dead, Her last disorder
mortal.

Oliver Goldsmith
Irish-born British writer.

51 Doctors think a lot of patients are cured who have simply
quit in disgust.

Don Herold

52 What I call a good patient is one who, having
found a good physician, sticks to him till he
dies.

Oliver Wendell Holmes (1809–94)
US writer.

53   Doctors will have more lives to answer for in the next world than even we generals.

Napoleon I (Napoleon Bonaparte; 1769–1821)
French Emperor.

54   A young doctor makes a humpy graveyard.

Proverb

55   There are worse occupations in this world than feeling a woman's pulse.

Laurence Sterne (1713–68)
Irish-born British writer.

56   He has been a doctor a year now and has had two patients, no, three, I think – yes, it was three; I attended their funerals.

Mark Twain (Samuel Langhorne Clemens; 1835–1910)
US writer.

57   Doctors are men who prescribe medicines of which they know little, to cure diseases of which they know less, in human beings of whom they know nothing.

Voltaire (François-Marie Arouet; 1694–1778)
French writer.

EDITORS

58   Where were you fellows when the paper was blank?

Fred Allen (1894–1956)
US comedian.
Said to writers who heavily edited one of his scripts

59   An editor should have a pimp for a brother, so he'd have somebody to look up to.

Gene Fowler (1890–1960)
US author.

60 There are just two people entitled to refer to themselves as "we"; one is a newspaper editor and the other is a fellow with a tapeworm.

Bill Nye

61 An editor is one who separates the wheat from the chaff and prints the chaff.

Adlai Stevenson (1900–65)
US statesman.

FARMERS

62 Our Farmers round, well pleased with constant gain,
Like other farmers, flourish and complain.

George Crabbe (1754–1832)
British poet.

63 A good farmer is nothing more nor less than a handy man with a sense of humus.

E. B. White (1899–1985)
US journalist and humorist.

JOURNALISTS

64 Doctors bury their mistakes. Lawyers hang them.
But journalists put theirs on the front
page.

Anonymous

65 'Christianity, of course but why journalism?'

Arthur Balfour (1848–1930)
British statesman.
In reply to Frank Harris's remark, '…all the faults of the age come
from Christianity and journalism'

66   It was long ago in my life as a simple reporter that I
decided that facts must never get in the way of truth.

James Cameron (1911–85)
British journalist.

67   Journalism largely consists of saying 'Lord Jones is dead'
to people who never knew Lord Jones was alive.

G. K. Chesterton (1874–1936)
British writer.

68   Literature is the art of writing something that will be read
twice; journalism what will be grasped at once.

Cyril Connolly (1903–74)
British journalist.

69   Once a newspaper touches a story, the facts are lost
forever, even to the protagonists.

Norman Mailer (1923–)
US writer.

70   A good newspaper, I suppose, is a nation talking to itself.

Arthur Miller (1915–)
US dramatist.

71   A reporter is a man who has renounced everything in life
but the world, the flesh, and the devil.

David Murray (1888–1962)
British journalist.

72 He's someone who flies around from hotel to hotel and thinks the most interesting thing about any story is the fact that he has arrived to cover it.

Tom Stoppard (1937–)
Czech-born British dramatist.
Referring to foreign correspondents

73 There is much to be said in favour of modern journalism. By giving us the opinions of the uneducated, it keeps us in touch with the ignorance of the community.

Oscar Wilde (1854–1900)
Irish-born British dramatist.

JUDGES

74 The duty of a judge is to administer justice, but his practice is to delay it.

Jean de La Bruyère (1645–96)
French satirist.

75 A judge is a law student who marks his own examination papers.

H. L. Mencken (1880–1956)
US journalist.

76 A judge is not supposed to know anything about the facts of life until they have been presented in evidence and explained to him at least three times.

Hubert Lister Parker (1900–72)
Lord Chief Justice of England.

77 Judges, like the criminal classes, have their lighter moments.

Oscar Wilde (1854–1900)
Irish-born British dramatist.

LAWYERS

78 A solicitor is a man who calls in a person he doesn't know
to sign a contract he hasn't seen to buy property he
doesn't want with money he hasn't got.

Dingwall Bateson (1898–1967)
President of the Law Society, 1952–53.

79 There is the prostitute, one who lets out her body for hire.
A dreadful thing, but are we ourselves so innocent? Do
not lawyers, for instance, let out their brains for hire?

Lord Brabazon (1884–1964)
British motorist, aviator, and politician.

80 If there were no bad people there would be no good
lawyers.

Charles Dickens (1812–70)
British novelist.

81 God works wonders now and then;
Behold a lawyer, an honest man.

Benjamin Franklin (1706–90)
US scientist and statesman.

82 Lawyers earn a living by the sweat of their browbeating.

James G. Huneker

83 I think we may class the lawyer in the natural history of
monsters.

John Keats (1795–1821)
British poet.

84 It is unfair to believe everything we hear about lawyers – some of it might not be true.

Gerald F. Lieberman

85 It has been said that the course to be pursued by a lawyer was first to get on, second to get honour, and third to get honest.

George M. Palmer

86 A good lawyer is a bad neighbour.

Proverb

87 A lawyer without history or literature is a mechanic, a mere working mason; if he possesses some knowledge of these, he may venture to call himself an architect.

Walter Scott (1771–1832)
Scottish novelist.

INSURANCE AGENTS

88 I detest life-insurance agents. They always argue that I shall some day die, which is not so.

Stephen Leacock (1869–1944)
English-born Canadian economist and humorist.

POLICE

89 I have never seen a situation so dismal that a policeman couldn't make it worse.

Brendan Behan (1923–64)
Irish playwright.

90 I'm not against the police; I'm just afraid of them.

Alfred Hitchcock (1899–1980)
British film director.

91   Policemen are numbered in case they get lost.

Spike Milligan (1918–)
British comic actor and author.

92   My father didn't create you to arrest me.

Lord Peel (1829–1912)
British politician.
Protesting against his arrest by the police, recently established by his
father

POLITICIANS

93   Your politicians will always be there when they need you.

Anonymous
US T-shirt slogan

94   The art of looking for trouble, finding it whether it exists
or not, diagnosing it incorrectly, and applying the wrong
remedy.

Ernest Benn (1875–1954)
British publisher.
Defining the art of politics

95   If a traveller were informed that such a man was leader of
the House of Commons, he may well begin to compre-
hend how the Egyptians worshipped an insect.

Benjamin Disraeli (1804–81)
British statesman.
Referring to Lord John Russell

96   The first rule of politics is not to lie to somebody unless it
is absolutely necessary.

Russell B. Long (1918–)
US lawyer and politician.

97 When you're abroad you're a statesman: when you're at home you're just a politician.

Harold Macmillan (1894–1986)
British statesman.

98 I used to say that politics was the second lowest profession and I have come to know that it bears a great similarity to the first.

Ronald Reagan (1911–)
US politician and president.

99 Nixon is the kind of politician who would cut down a redwood tree, then mount the stump for a conservation speech.

Adlai Stevenson (1900–65)
US statesman.

100 Any woman who understands the problems of running a home will be nearer to understanding the problems of running a country.

Margaret Thatcher (1925–)
British politician and prime minister.

101 Politics is the art of preventing people from taking part in affairs which properly concern them.

Paul Valéry (1871–1945)
French poet and writer.

102 Any American who is prepared to run for President should automatically, by definition, be disqualified from ever doing so.

Gore Vidal (1925–)
US novelist.

103 Politics come from man. Mercy, compassion and justice come from God.

Terry Waite (1939–)
British churchman.

PSYCHIATRISTS

104 Psychiatrist: A man who asks you a lot of expensive questions your wife asks you for nothing.

Sam Bardell (1915–)

105 The trouble with Freud is that he never played the Glasgow Empire Saturday night.

Ken Dodd (1931–)
British comedian.

106 One should only see a psychiatrist out of boredom.

Muriel Spark (1918–)
British novelist.

107 A psychiatrist is a man who goes to the Folies-Bergère and looks at the audience.

Mervyn Stockwood (1913–95)
British churchman.

SERVANTS

108 Here are all kinds of employers wanting all sorts of servants, and all sorts of servants wanting all kinds of employers, and they never seem to come together.

Charles Dickens (1812–70)
British novelist.

109 The difference between a man and his valet; they both smoke the same cigars, but only one pays for them.

Robert Frost (1875–1963)
US poet.

110 A good servant is a real godsend; but truly 'tis a rare bird in the land.

Martin Luther (1483–1546)
German Protestant.

THE SERVICES

111 Soldiers in peace are like chimneys in summer.

William Cecil, Lord Burghley (1520–98)
English statesman.

112 Drinking is the soldier's pleasure.

John Dryden (1631–1700)
British poet and dramatist.

113 The wonder is always new that any sane man can be a sailor.

Ralph Waldo Emerson (1803–82)
US poet and essayist.

114 No man will be a sailor who has contrivance enough to get himself into a jail; for being in a ship is being in a jail, with the chance of being drowned…A man in a jail has more room, better food and commonly better company.

Samuel Johnson (1709–84)
British lexicographer.

115 It's Tommy this, an' Tommy that, an' 'Chuck him out, the brute!'

But it's 'Saviour of 'is country' when the guns begin to shoot.

Rudyard Kipling (1865–1936)
Indian-born British writer.

116 The worse the man the better the soldier. If soldiers be not corrupt they out to be made so.

Napoleon I (Napoleon Bonaparte; 1769–1821)
French emperor.

117 When the military man approaches, the world locks up its spoons and packs off its womankind.

George Bernard Shaw (1856–1950)
Irish dramatist and critic.

118 We sailors get money like horses, and spent it like asses.

Tobias Smollett (1721–71)
British novelist.

119 He (the recruiting officer) asked me 'Why tanks?' I replied that I preferred to go into battle sitting down.

Peter Ustinov (1921–)
British actor.

120 I don't know what effect these men will have on the enemy, but, by God, they frighten me.

Duke of Wellington (1769–1852)
British general and statesman.
Referring to his generals

TEACHERS

121 A teacher affects eternity.

Henry B. Adams (1838–1918)
US historian.

122 The true teacher defends his pupils against his own personal influence.

A. B. Alcott (1799–1888)
US writer.

123 Being a professor of poetry is rather like being a Kentucky colonel. It's not really a subject one can profess – unless one hires oneself out to write pieces for funerals or the marriages of dons.

W. H. Auden (1907–73)
British poet.

124 A schoolmaster should have an atmosphere of awe, and walk wonderingly, as if he was amazed at being himself.

Walter Bagehot (1826–77)
British economist and journalist.

125 It were better to perish than to continue schoolmastering.

Thomas Carlyle (1795–1881)
Scottish historian and essayist.

126 Headmasters have powers at their disposal with which Prime Ministers have never yet been invested.

Winston Churchill (1874–1965)
British statesman.

127 It is the supreme art of the teacher to awaken joy in creative expression and knowledge.

Albert Einstein (1879–1955)
German-born US physicist.

128 One looks back with appreciation to the brilliant teachers, but with gratitude to those who touched our human feelings. The curriculum is so much necessary raw material, but warmth is the vital element for the growing plant and for the soul of the child.

Carl Gustav Jung (1875–1961)
Swiss psychoanalyst.

129 Therefore for the love of God appoint teachers and schoolmasters, you that have the charge of youth; and give the teachers stipends worthy of the pains.

Hugh Latimer (1485–1555)
English churchman.

130 The average schoolmaster is and always must be essentially an ass, for how can one imagine an intelligent man engaging in so puerile an avocation?

H. L. Mencken (1880–1956)
US journalist.

131 A teacher is one who, in his youth, admired teachers.

H. L. Mencken

132 I am inclined to think that one's education has been in vain if one fails to learn that most schoolmasters are idiots.

Hesketh Pearson (1887–1964)
British biographer.

133 A teacher should have maximal authority and minimal power.

Thomas Szasz (1920–)
US psychiatrist.

OPPORTUNITY

1 Opportunities are usually disguised as hard work, so most people don't recognise them.

Ann Landers (1918–)
US journalist.

2 One can present people with opportunities. One cannot make them equal to them.

Rosamond Lehmann (1901–90)
British novelist.

3 Equality of opportunity means equal opportunity to be unequal.

Iain Macleod (1913–70)
British politician.

OPTIMISM

1 The optimist proclaims we live in the best of all possible worlds; and the pessimist fears this is true.

James Cabell (1879–1958)
US novelist and journalist.

2 The latest definition of an optimist is one who fills up his crossword puzzle in ink.

Clement King Shorter (1857–1926)
British journalist and critic.

3 I am an optimist, unrepentant and militant. After all, in order not to be a fool an optimist must know how sad a place the world can be. It is only the pessimist who finds this out anew every day.

Peter Ustinov (1921–)
British actor.

ORIGINALITY

1 Anything that is worth doing has been done frequently. Things hitherto undone should be given, I suspect, a wide berth.

Max Beerbohm (1872–1956)
British writer.

2 An original writer is not one who imitates nobody, but one whom nobody can imitate.

Vicomte de Chateaubriand (1768–1848)
French diplomat and writer.

PARTIES

1 I entertained on a cruising trip that was so much fun that I had to sink my yacht to make my guests go home.

F. Scott Fitzgerald (1896–1940)
US novelist.

2 The best number for a dinner party is two – myself and a dam' good head waiter.

Nubar Gulbenkian (1896–1972)
Turkish oil magnate.

3 Certainly, there is nothing else here to enjoy.

George Bernard Shaw (1856–1950)
Irish dramatist and critic.
At a party when his hostess asked whether he was enjoying himself

PAST

1   We are always doing something for posterity, but I would fain see posterity do something for us.

Joseph Addison (1672–1719)
British essayist.

2   Even God cannot change the past.

Agathon (c. 446–401 BC)
Athenian poet and playwright.

3   The past is a foreign country: they do things differently there.

L. P. Hartley (1895–1972)
British novelist.

4   Look back, and smile at perils past.

Walter Scott (1771–1832)
Scottish novelist.

5   The past is the only dead thing that smells sweet.

Edward Thomas (1878–1917)
British poet.

6   Keep off your thoughts from things that are past and done;
For thinking of the past wakes regret and pain.

Arthur Waley (1889–1966)
British poet and translator.
Translation from the Chinese of Po-Chü-I

7   The past, at least, is secure.

Daniel Webster (1782–1852)
US statesman.

PATIENCE

1   Beware the Fury of a Patient Man.

John Dryden (1631–1700)
British poet and dramatist.

2   Very well, I can wait.

Arnold Schoenberg (1874–1951)
German composer.
Replying to a complaint that his violin concerto would need a musician
with six fingers. Attrib.

3   It is very strange…that the years teach us patience; that
the shorter our time, the greater our capacity for waiting.

Elizabeth Taylor (1912–75)
British writer.

PATRIOTISM

1   Our country! In her intercourse with foreign nations, may
she always be in the right; but our country, right or
wrong.

Stephen Decatur (1779–1820)
US naval officer.

2   Patriotism is the last refuge of a scoundrel.

Samuel Johnson (1709–84)
British lexicographer.

PEACE

1   *Peace,* n. In international affairs, a period of cheating
between two periods of fighting.

Ambrose Bierce (1842–?1914)
US writer and journalist.

2 Arms alone are not enough to keep the peace – it must be kept by men.

John Fitzgerald Kennedy (1917–63)
US statesman.

3 The issues are the same. We wanted peace on earth, love, and understanding between everyone around the world. We have learned that change comes slowly.

Paul McCartney (1943–)
British rock musician.

4 We prepare for war like ferocious giants, and for peace like retarded pygmies.

Lester Pearson (1897–1972)
Canadian politician.

PERFECTION

1 Perfection has one grave defect; it is apt to be dull.

W. Somerset Maugham (1874–1965)
British novelist.

PESSIMISM

1 The optimist proclaims we live in the best of all possible worlds; and the pessimist fears this is true.

James Cabell (1879–1958)
US novelist and journalist.

2 If we see light at the end of the tunnel it is the light of an oncoming train.

Robert Lowell (1917–77)
US poet.

3   How many pessimists end up by desiring the things they fear, in order to prove that they are right.

Robert Mallet (1915–)
French writer.

4   A pessimist is a man who looks both ways before crossing a one-way street.

Laurence J. Peter (1919–90)
Canadian writer.

PHILOSOPHY

1   The point of philosophy is to start with something so simple as to seem not worth stating, and to end with something so paradoxical that no one will believe it.

Bertrand Russell (1872–1970)
British philosopher.

2   It is a great advantage for a system of philosophy to be substantially true.

George Santayana (1863–1952)
US philosopher.

3   My advice to you is not to inquire why or whither, but just enjoy your ice-cream while it's on your plate – that's my philosophy.

Thornton Wilder (1897–1975)
US novelist and dramatist.

PLACES

1   Streets full of water. Please advise.

Robert Benchley (1889–1945)
US humorist.
Telegram sent to his editor on arriving in Venice

2   Well, the principle seems the same. The water still keeps falling over.

Winston Churchill (1874–1965)
British statesman.
When asked whether the Niagara Falls looked the same as when he first saw them

3   The Almighty in His infinite wisdom did not see fit to create Frenchmen in the image of Englishmen.

Winston Churchill

4   India is a geographical term. It is no more a united nation than the Equator.

Winston Churchill

5   I cannot forecast to you the action of Russia. It is a riddle wrapped in a mystery inside an enigma.

Winston Churchill

6   Latins are tenderly enthusiastic. In Brazil they throw flowers at you. In Argentina they throw themselves.

Marlene Dietrich (Maria Magdalene von Losch; 1904–92)
German-born film star.

7   If you are lucky enough to have lived in Paris as a young man, then wherever you go for the rest of your life, it stays with you, for Paris is a moveable feast.

Ernest Hemingway (1899–1961)
US novelist.

8 Dublin, though a place much worse than London, is not so bad as Iceland.

Samuel Johnson (1709–84)
British lexicographer.

9 Cusins is a very nice fellow, certainly: nobody would ever guess that he was born in Australia.

George Bernard Shaw (1856–1950)
Irish dramatist and critic.

PLEASURE

1 One half of the world cannot understand the pleasures of the other.

Jane Austen (1775–1817)
British novelist.

2 Life would be tolerable, were it not for its amusements.

George Cornewall Lewis (1806–63)
British statesman and writer.

3 All the things I really like to do are either immoral, illegal, or fattening.

Alexander Woollcott (1887–1943)
US journalist.

POPULARITY

1 Everybody hates me because I'm so universally liked.

Peter De Vries (1910–93)
US novelist.

2 He hasn't an enemy in the world, and none of his friends like him.

Oscar Wilde (1854–1900)
Irish-born British dramatist.
Said of G. B. Shaw

POVERTY

1 The trouble with being poor is that it takes up all your time.

Willem de Kooning (1904–97)
US artist.

2 It is only the poor who are forbidden to beg.

Anatole France (Jacques Anatole François Thibault; 1844–1924)
French writer.

3 Look at me: I worked my way up from nothing to a state of extreme poverty.

Groucho Marx (Julius Marx; 1895–1977)
US comedian.

4 Whereas it has long been known and declared that the poor have no right to the property of the rich, I wish it also to be known and declared that the rich have no right to the property of the poor.

John Ruskin (1819–1900)
British art critic and writer.

5 When the rich wage war it is the poor who die.

Jean-Paul Sartre (1905–80)
French writer.

6 There were times my pants were so thin I could sit on a dime and tell if it was heads or tails.

Spencer Tracy (1900–67)
US film star.

POWER

1 Power tends to corrupt, and absolute power corrupts
absolutely. Great men are almost always bad men...There
is no worse heresy than that the office sanctifies the
holder of it.

Lord Acton (1834–1902)
British historian.
Often misquoted as 'Power corrupts...'

2 He did not care in which direction the car was travelling,
so long as he remained in the driver's seat.

Lord Beaverbrook (1879–1964)
Canadian-born British newspaper proprietor.
Referring to Lloyd George

3 Being powerful is like being a lady. If you have to tell
people you are, you ain't.

Jesse Carr

4 There is one thing about being President – nobody can
tell you when to sit down.

Dwight D. Eisenhower (1890–1969)
US general and statesman.

5 Men of power have not time to read; yet men who do not
read are unfit for power.

Michael Foot (1913–)
British Labour politician and journalist.

6 People have power when other people think they have
power.

William Wyche Fowler (1940–)
US politician.

7 You only have power over people so long as you don't take *everything* away from them. But when you've robbed a man of everything he's no longer in your power – he's free again.

Alexander Solzhenitsyn (1918–)
Russian novelist.

8 God is always on the side of the big battalions.

Vicomte de Turenne (1611–75)
French marshal.

9 God is on the side not of the heavy battalions, but of the best shots.

Voltaire (François-Marie Arouet; 1694–1778)
French writer.

10 The wrong sort of people are always in power because they would not be in power if they were not the wrong sort of people.

Jon Wynne-Tyson (1924–)
British humorous writer.

PRACTICALITY

1 Don't carry away that arm till I have taken off my ring.

Lord Raglan (1788–1855)
British field marshal.
Request immediately after his arm had been amputated following the battle of Waterloo

2 Very well, then I shall not take off my boots.

Duke of Wellington (1769–1852)
British general and statesman.
Responding to the news, as he was going to bed, that the ship in which
he was travelling seemed about to sink

PRAISE

1 Watch how a man takes praise and there you have the
measure of him.

Thomas Burke (1886–1945)
British writer.

2 The advantage of doing one's praising for oneself is that
one can lay it on so thick and exactly in the right places.

Samuel Butler (1835–1902)
British writer.

3 To refuse praise reveals a desire to be praised twice over.

Duc de la Rochefoucauld (1613–80)
French writer.

PRAYER

1 The idea that He would take his attention away from the
universe in order to give me a bicycle with three speeds is
just so unlikely I can't go along with it.

Quentin Crisp (c. 1910–)
British model, publicist, and writer.

2 Forgive, O Lord, my little jokes on Thee
And I'll forgive Thy great big one on me.

Robert Frost (1875–1963)
US poet.

3 I am just going to pray for you at St Paul's, but with no
very lively hope of success.

Sydney Smith (1771–1845)
British clergyman and essayist.
On meeting an acquaintance

PREJUDICE

1 Mother is far too clever to understand anything she does not like.

Arnold Bennett (1867–1931)
British novelist.

2 Common sense is the collection of prejudices acquired by age eighteen.

Albert Einstein (1879–1955)
German-born US physicist.

PRESENT

1 Gather ye rosebuds while ye may,
Old time is still a-flying:
And this same flower that smiles today
Tomorrow will be dying.

Robert Herrick (1591–1674)
English poet.

2 Drop the question what tomorrow may bring, and count as profit every day that Fate allows you.

Horace (Quintus Horatius Flaccus; 65–8 BC)
Roman poet.

PRIDE

1 I know of no case where a man added to his dignity by standing on it.

Winston Churchill (1874–1965)
British politician. Attrib.

2 When you have a great cause to fight for, the moment of greatest humiliation is the moment when the spirit is proudest.

Christabel Pankhurst (1880–1958)
British suffragette.

PRINCIPLES

1 It is easier to fight for one's principles than to live up to them.

Alfred Adler (1870–1937)
Austrian psychiatrist.

2 You must learn that there are times when a man in public life is compelled to rise above his principles.

Henry S. Ashurst
US politician.

3 Whenever two good people argue over principles, they are both right.

Marie Ebner von Eschenbach (1830–1916)
Austrian writer.

4 Nobody ever did anything very foolish except from some strong principle.

Lord Melbourne (1779–1848)
British statesman.

PROGRESS

1 The people who live in the past must yield to the people who live in the future. Otherwise the world would begin to turn the other way round.

Arnold Bennett (1867–1931)
British novelist.

2 All progress is based upon a universal innate desire on the part of every organism to live beyond its income.

Samuel Butler (1835–1902)
British writer.

3 What we call progress is the exchange of one nuisance for another nuisance.

Havelock Ellis (1859–1939)
British sexologist.

4 All that is human must retrograde if it does not advance.

Edward Gibbon (1737–94)
British historian.

5 You cannot fight against the future. Time is on our side.

William Ewart Gladstone (1809–98)
British statesman.
Advocating parliamentary reform

6 If I have seen further it is by standing on the shoulders of giants.

Isaac Newton (1642–1727)
British scientist.

PROMISES

1 Better is it that thou shouldest not vow, than that thou shouldest vow and not pay.

Bible: Ecclesiastes

2 A promise made is a debt unpaid.

Robert William Service (1874–1958)
Canadian poet.

PROMPTNESS

1 Punctuality is the politeness of kings.

Louis XVIII (1755–1824)
French king.

2 Punctuality is the virtue of the bored.

Evelyn Waugh (1903–66)
British novelist.

PRONUNCIATION

1 Everybody has a right to pronounce foreign names as he chooses.

Winston Churchill (1874–1965)
British statesman.

PROPHECY

1 Mr Turnbull had predicted evil consequences...and was

now doing the best in his power to bring about the verification of his own prophecies.

Anthony Trollope (1815–82)
British novelist.

PRUDENCE

1   One does not insult the river god while crossing the river.

Anonymous
Chinese proverb

2   Put your trust in God, my boys, and keep your powder dry.

Valentine Blacker (1778–1823)
British soldier.

3   I'm an optimist, but I'm an optimist who carries a raincoat.

Harold Wilson (1916–95)
British politician and prime minister.

PUBLIC

1   You cannot make a man by standing a sheep on its hind legs. But by standing a flock of sheep in that position you can make a crowd of men.

Max Beerbohm (1872–1956)
British writer.

2   The Public is an old woman. Let her maunder and mumble.

Thomas Carlyle (1795–1881)
Scottish historian and essayist.

3   The people would be just as noisy if they were going to
    see me hanged.

    Oliver Cromwell (1599–1658)
    English soldier and statesman.
    Referring to a cheering crowd

4   There is not a more mean, stupid, dastardly, pitiful,
    selfish, spiteful, envious, ungrateful animal than the
    public. It is the greatest of cowards, for it is afraid of itself.

    William Hazlitt (1778–1830)
    British essayist.

5   Only constant repetition will finally succeed in imprinting
    an idea on the memory of the crowd.

    Adolf Hitler (1889–1945)
    German dictator.

6   The people long eagerly for just two things – bread and
    circuses.

    Juvenal (Decimus Junius Juvenalis; 60–130 AD)
    Roman satirist.

PURITY

1   I'm as pure as the driven slush.

    Tallulah Bankhead (1903–68)
    US actress.

2   I thought of losing my virginity as a career move.

    Madonna (Madonna Louise Ciccone; 1958–)
    US singer and actress.

3   Caesar's wife must be above suspicion.

    Proverb

4   It is one of the superstitions of the human mind to have
    imagined that virginity could be a virtue.

Voltaire (François-Marie Arouet; 1694–1778)
French writer.

5   I used to be Snow White...but I drifted.

Mae West (1892–1980)
US actress.

QUOTATIONS

1   It is gentlemanly to get one's quotations very slightly
wrong. In that way one unprigs onself and allows the
company to correct one.

Lord Ribblesdale (1854–1925)
British aristocrat.

REALISM

1   If at first you don't succeed, try, try again. Then quit. No
use being a damn fool about it.

W. C. Fields (1880–1946)
US actor.

REGRET

1   Were it not better to forget
Than but remember and regret?

Letitia Landon (1802–38)
British poet and novelist.

2   The follies which a man regrets most in his life are those
which he didn't commit when he had the opportunity.

Helen Rowland (1876–1950)
US writer.

3   What's gone and what's past help
    Should be past grief.

    William Shakespeare (1564–1616)
    English dramatist.

RELIGION

1   The Jews and Arabs should sit down and settle their
    differences like good Christians.

    Warren Austin (1877–1962)
    US politician and diplomat.

2   One cathedral is worth a hundred theologians capable of
    proving the existence of God by logic.

    Julian Barnes (1946–)
    British novelist.

3   As for the British churchman, he goes to church as he
    goes to the bathroom, with the minimum of fuss and no
    explanation if he can help it.

    Ronald Blythe (1922–)
    British writer.

4   The idea that only a male can represent Christ at the altar
    is a most serious heresy.

    Dr George Carey (1935–)
    British churchman and Archbishop of Canterbury.

5   There exists no politician in India daring enough to
    attempt to explain to the masses that cows can be eaten.

    Indira Gandhi (1917–84)
    Indian stateswoman.

6   When the white man came we had the land and they had

the Bibles; now they have the land and we have the Bibles.

Dan George (1899–1982)
Canadian Indian chief.

REPUTATION

1   I hold it as certain, that no man was ever written out of reputation but by himself.

Richard Bentley (1662–1742)
English academic.

2   Until you've lost your reputation, you never realize what a burden it was or what freedom really is.

Margaret Mitchell (1909–49)
US novelist.

RESPONSIBILITY

1   Perhaps it is better to be irresponsible and right than to be responsible and wrong.

Winston Churchill (1874–1965)
British statesman.

2   The buck stops here.

Harry S. Truman (1884–1972)
US statesman.
Sign kept on his desk during his term as president

3   In dreams begins responsibility.

W. B. Yeats (1865–1939)
Irish poet.

RIDICULE

1 Few women care to be laughed at and men not at all, except for large sums of money.

Alan Ayckbourn (1939–)
British dramatist.

RIGHT

1 This the grave of Mike O'Day
Who died maintaining his right of way.
His right was clear, his will was strong.
But he's just as dead as if he'd been wrong.

Anonymous

2 Always do right. This will gratify some people, and astonish the rest.

Mark Twain (Samuel Langhorne Clemens; 1835–1910)
US writer.

ROYALTY

1 Her Majesty is not a subject.

Benjamin Disraeli (1804–81)
British statesman.
Responding to Gladstone's taunt that Disraeli could make a joke out of any subject, including Queen Victoria

2 It has none, your Highness. Its history dates from today.

James Whistler (1834–1903)
US painter.
Replying to a query from the Prince of Wales about the history of the Society of British Artists, which he was visiting for the first time

RUTHLESSNESS

1 We are programmed (by biology or conditioning – who cares which?) to respond to social signals and pressures, and so find it almost impossible to be as single-mindedly ruthless as men.

Janet Daley
British journalist.

2 I do not have to forgive my enemies, I have had them all shot.

Ramón Maria Narváez (1800–68)
Spanish general and political leader.
Said on his deathbed, when asked by a priest if he forgave his enemies

3 It is not enough to succeed. Others must fail.

Gore Vidal (1925–)
US novelist.

SARCASM

1 If you don't want to use the army, I should like to borrow it for a while. Yours respectfully,
A. Lincoln.

Abraham Lincoln (1809–65)
US statesman.
Letter to General George B. McClellan, whose lack of activity during the US Civil War irritated Lincoln

SCEPTICISM

1 We don't believe in rheumatism and true love until after the first attack.

Marie Ebner von Eschenbach (1830–1916)
Austrian writer.

2   I am too much of a sceptic to deny the possibility of anything.

T. H. Huxley (1825–95)
British biologist.

SCIENCE

1   It is, of course, a bit of a drawback that science was invented after I left school.

Lord Carrington (1919–)
British statesman.

2   For him, truth is so seldom the sudden light that shows new order and beauty; more often, truth is the uncharted rock that sinks his ship in the dark.

John Cornforth (1917–)
Australian chemist.
On the scientist in his search for truth

3   When you are courting a nice girl an hour seems like a second. When you sit on a red-hot cinder a second seems like an hour. That's relativity.

Albert Einstein (1879–1955)
German-born US physicist.

4   A science is said to be useful if its development tends to accentuate the existing inequalities of wealth, or more directly promotes the destruction of human life.

Godfrey Harold Hardy (1877–1947)
British mathematician.

5   The airplane stays up because it doesn't have the time to fall.

Orville Wright (1871–1948)
US aviator.
Explaining the principles of powered flight

SCOTLAND

1 There are few more impressive sights in the world than a Scotsman on the make.

J. M. Barrie (1860–1937)
British playwright.

2 Much may be made of a Scotchman, if he be *caught* young.

Samuel Johnson (1701–84)
British lexicographer.
Referring to Lord Mansfield

3 Their learning is like bread in a besieged town: every man gets a little, but no man gets a full meal.

Samuel Johnson
Referring to education in Scotland

4 It is never difficult to distinguish between a Scotsman with a grievance and a ray of sunshine.

P. G. Wodehouse (1881–1975)
British humorous novelist.

SECRECY

1 I know that's a secret, for it's whispered every where.

William Congreve (1670–1729)
British Restoration dramatist.

2 It is a secret in the Oxford sense: you may tell it to only one person at a time.

Oliver Franks (1905–92)
British philosopher and administrator.

SELF-CONFIDENCE

1   I know I'm not clever but I'm always right.

    J. M. Barrie (1860–1937)
    British playwright.

2   I think I'm getting a little confidence now.

    John Gielgud (1904–)
    British actor.
    Remark made at the age of 71

3   As for conceit, what man will do any good who is not
conceited? Nobody holds a good opinion of a man who
has a low opinion of himself.

    Anthony Trollope (1815–82)
    British novelist.

SELF-CONTROL

1   When things are steep, remember to stay level-headed.

    Horace (Quintus Horatius Flaccus; 65–8 BC)
    Roman poet.

2   If you can keep your head when all about you
Are losing theirs and blaming it on you.

    Rudyard Kipling (1865–1936)
    Indian-born British writer.

SELFISHNESS

1   The least pain in our little finger gives us more concern

and uneasiness than the destruction of millions of our
fellow-beings.

William Hazlitt (1778–1830)
British essayist.

2   It is difficult to love mankind unless one has a reasonable
private income and when one has a reasonable private
income one has better things to do than loving mankind.

Hugh Kingsmill (1889–1949)
British writer.

SELFLESSNESS

1   To give and not to count the cost;
To fight and not to heed the wounds;
To toil and not to seek for rest;
To labour and not ask for any reward
Save that of knowing that we do Thy will.

St Ignatius Loyola (1491–1556)
Spanish priest.

SELF-MADE MEN

1   I know he is, and he adores his maker.

Benjamin Disraeli (1804–81)
British statesman.
Replying to a remark made in defence of John Bright that he was a
self-made man

2   He was a self-made man who owed his lack of success to
nobody.

Joseph Heller (1923–99)
US novelist.

3   A self-made man is one who believes in luck and sends his son to Oxford.

Christina Stead (1902–83)
Australian novelist.

SELF-PRESERVATION

1   This animal is very bad; when attacked it defends itself.

Anonymous

SELF-RELIANCE

1   I thank God that I am endued with such qualities that if I were turned out of the Realm in my petticoat I were able to live in any place in Christome.

Elizabeth I (1533–1603)
Queen of England.

2   I'll never
Be such a gosling to obey instinct, but stand
As if a man were author of himself
And knew no other kin.

William Shakespeare (1564–1616)
English dramatist.

SENTIMENTALITY

1   One may not regard the world as a sort of metaphysical brothel for emotion.

Arthur Koestler (1905–83)
Hungarian-born British writer.

2 Sentimentality is only sentiment that rubs you up the wrong way.

W. Somerset Maugham (1874–1965)
British novelist.

SERIOUSNESS

1 Angels can fly because they take themselves lightly.

G. K. Chesterton (1874–1936)
British writer.

SERVICE

1 God doth not need
Either man's work or his own gifts. Who best
Bear his mild yoke, they serve him best; his state
Is kingly; thousands at his bidding speed,
And post o'er land and ocean without rest;
They also serve who only stand and wait.

John Milton (1608–74)
English poet.

2 Small service is true service, while it lasts.

William Wordsworth (1770–1850)
British poet.

SEX

1 My brain: it's my second favourite organ.

Woody Allen (Allen Stewart Konigsberg; 1935–)
US film actor.

2   It was the most fun I ever had without laughing.

Woody Allen

3   Money, it turned out, was exactly like sex, you thought of nothing else if you didn't have it and thought of other things if you did.

James Baldwin (1924–87)
US writer.

4   When she raises her eyelids it's as if she were taking off all her clothes.

Colette (1873–1954)
French novelist.

5   I see – she's the original good time that was had by all.

Bette Davis (Ruth Elizabeth Davis; 1908–89)
US film star.
Referring to a starlet of the time

6   Personally I know nothing about sex because I've always been married.

Zsa Zsa Gabor (1919–)
Hungarian-born US film star.

7   Sexual intercourse began
In nineteen sixty-three
(Which was rather late for me) –
Between the end of the *Chatterley* ban
And the Beatles' first LP.

Philip Larkin (1922–85)
British poet.

8   If sex is such a natural phenomenon, how come there are so many books on how to?

Bette Midler (1944–)
US actress and comedienne.

9 You know, she speaks eighteen languages. And she can't say 'No' in any of them.

Dorothy Parker (1893–1967)
US writer.
Speaking of an acquaintance

10 All this fuss about sleeping together. For physical pleasure I'd sooner go to my dentist any day.

Evelyn Waugh (1903–66)
British novelist.

11 I'm glad you like my Catherine. I like her too. She ruled thirty million people and had three thousand lovers. I do the best I can in two hours.

Mae West (1892–1980)
US actress.
After her performance in *Catherine the Great*

12 It's not the men in my life that count; it's the life in my men.

Mae West

13 When I'm good I'm very good, but when I'm bad I'm better.

Mae West

SHYNESS

1 Shyness is just egotism out of its depth

Penelope Keith
British actress.

2 I have never known a *truly* modest person to be the least bit shy.

Elizabeth Taylor (1912–75)
British writer.

SIMPLICITY

1 A child of five would understand this.
Send somebody to fetch a child of five.

Groucho Marx (Julius Marx; 1895–1977)
US comedian.

SIN

1 All sin tends to be addictive, and the terminal point of addiction is what is called damnation.

W. H. Auden (1907–73)
British poet.

2 Don't tell my mother I'm living in sin,
Don't let the old folks know;
Don't tell my twin that I breakfast on gin,
He'd never survive the blow.

A. P. Herbert (1890–1971)
British writer.

SINCERITY

1 What comes from the heart, goes to the heart.

Samuel Taylor Coleridge (1772–1834)
British poet.

2 I'm afraid of losing my obscurity. Genuineness only thrives in the dark. Like celery.

Aldous Huxley (1894–1964)
British novelist.

3 What's a man's first duty? The answer's brief:
To be himself.

Henrik Ibsen (1828–1906)
Norwegian dramatist.

SLEEP

1 Laugh and the world laughs with you; snore and you sleep alone.

Anthony Burgess (1917–93)
British novelist and critic.

SMOKING

1 Certainly not – if you don't object if I'm sick.

Thomas Beecham (1879–1961)
British conductor.
When asked whether he minded if someone smoked in a non-smoking compartment

2 I must point out that my rule of life prescribed as an absolutely sacred rite smoking cigars and also the drinking of alcohol before, after, and if need be during all meals and in the intervals between them.

Winston Churchill (1874–1965)
British statesman.
Said during a lunch with the Arab leader Ibn Saud, when he heard that the king's religion forbade smoking and alcohol

3 A custom loathsome to the eye, hateful to the nose,

harmful to the brain, dangerous to the lungs, and in the black, stinking fume thereof, nearest resembling the horrible Stygian smoke of the pit that is bottomless.

James I (1566–1625)
King of England.

4   He who lives without tobacco is not worthy to live.

Molière (Jean Baptiste Poquelin; 1622–73)
French dramatist.

5   This vice brings in one hundred million francs in taxes every year. I will certainly forbid it at once – as soon as you can name a virtue that brings in as much revenue.

Napoleon III (1808–73)
French emperor.
Reply when asked to ban smoking

SNOBBERY

1   Of course they have, or I wouldn't be sitting here talking to someone like you.

Barbara Cartland (1902–)
British romantic novelist.
When asked in a radio interview whether she thought that British class barriers had broken down

2   I mustn't go on singling out names. One must not be a name-dropper, as Her Majesty remarked to me yesterday.

Norman St John Stevas (1929–)
British politician.

3   She was – but I assure you that she was a very bad cook.

Louis Adolphe Thiers (1797–1877)
French statesman and historian.
Defending his social status after someone had remarked that his
mother had been a cook

SOCIETY

1 Man is a social animal.

Benedict Spinoza (Baruch de Spinoza; 1632–77)
Dutch philosopher.

2 What men call social virtues, good fellowship, is
commonly but the virtue of pigs in a litter, which lie close
together to keep each other warm.

Henry David Thoreau (1817–62)
US writer.

SOLITUDE

1 A man must keep a little back shop where he can be
himself without reserve. In solitude alone can he know
true freedom.

Michel de Montaigne (1533–92)
French essayist.

SORROW

1 One often calms one's grief by recounting it.

Pierre Corneille (1606–84)
French dramatist.

2 The secret of being miserable is to have leisure to bother
about whether you are happy or not.

George Bernard Shaw (1856–1950)
Irish dramatist and critic.

SPEECH

1   *Bore,* n. A person who talks when you wish him to listen.

Ambrose Bierce (1842–?1914)
US writer and journalist.

2   Oaths are but words, and words but wind.

Samuel Butler (1612–80)
English satirist.

3   When you have nothing to say, say nothing.

Charles Caleb Colton (?1780–1832)
British clergyman and writer.

4   No, Sir, because I have time to think before I speak, and don't ask impertinent questions.

Erasmus Darwin (1731–1802)
British physician, biologist, and poet.
Reply when asked whether he found his stammer inconvenient

5   You can stroke people with words.

F. Scott Fitzgerald (1896–1940)
US novelist.

6   The true use of speech is not so much to express our wants as to conceal them.

Oliver Goldsmith (1728–74)
Irish-born British writer.

7   Most men make little use of their speech than to give evidence against their own understanding.

Lord Halifax (1633–95)
English statesman.

8 That man's silence is wonderful to listen to.

Thomas Hardy (1840–1928)
British novelist.

9 Silence is as full of potential wisdom and wit as the unhewn marble of great sculpture.

Aldous Huxley (1894–1964)
British novelist.

10 Talking and eloquence are not the same: to speak, and to speak well, are two things.

Ben Jonson (1573–1637)
English dramatist.

11 Words are, of course, the most powerful drug used by mankind.

Rudyard Kipling (1865–1936)
Indian-born British writer.

12 Beware of the conversationalist who adds 'in other words'. He is merely starting afresh.

Robert Morley (1908–92)
British actor.

13 The most precious things in speech are pauses.

Ralph Richardson (1902–83)
British actor.

14 But words once spoke can never be recall'd.

Earl of Roscommon (1633–85)
Irish-born English poet.

15 He has occasional flashes of silence, that make his conversation perfectly delightful.

Sydney Smith (1771–1845)
British clergyman and essayist.
Referring to Lord Macaulay

16   A good listener is not someone who has nothing to say. A
good listener is a good talker with a sore throat.

Katherine Whitehorn (1926–)
British journalist.

SPORT

1   Golf is a game whose aim is to hit a very small ball into an
even smaller hole, with weapons singularly ill-designed
for the purpose.

Winston Churchill (1874–1965)
British statesman.

2   Exercise is bunk. If you are healthy, you don't need it: if
you are sick, you shouldn't take it.

Henry Ford (1863–1947)
US car manufacturer.

3   They came to see me bat not to see you bowl.

W. G. Grace (1848–1915)
British doctor and cricketer.
Refusing to leave the crease after being bowled first ball in front of a
large crowd

4   It's more than a game. It's an institution.

Thomas Hughes (1822–96)
British novelist.
Referring to cricket

5   Casting a ball at three straight sticks and defending the
same with a fourth.

Rudyard Kipling (1865–1936)
Indian-born British writer.

6   Golf may be played on Sunday, not being a game within
the view of the law, but being a form of moral effort.

Stephen Leacock (1869–1944)
English-born Canadian economist and humorist.

7   All I've got against it is that it takes you so far from the
club house.

Eric Linklater (1889–1974)
Scottish novelist.
Referring to golf

8   It is almost impossible to remember how tragic a place
the world is when one is playing golf.

Robert Lynd (1879–1949)
Irish essayist and journalist.

9   Football isn't a matter of life and death – it's much more
important than that.

Bill Shankly (1914–81)
British football manager.

10 I have always looked upon cricket as organised loafing.

William Temple (1881–1944)
British churchman.
Address to parents when headmaster of Repton School

11 Golf is a good walk spoiled.

Mark Twain (Samuel Langhorne Clemens; 1835–1910)
US writer.

12 There's no secret. You just press the accelerator to the
floor and steer left.

Bill Vukovich (1918–55)
US motor-racing driver.
Explaining his success in the Indianapolis 500

13 It requires one to assume such indecent postures.

Oscar Wilde (1854–1900)
Irish-born British dramatist.
Explaining why he did not play cricket

14 A day spent in a round of strenuous idleness.

William Wordsworth (1770–1850)
British poet.

STATISTICS

1 He uses statistics as a drunken man uses lamp-posts – for support rather than illumination.

Andrew Lang (1844–1912)
Scottish writer and poet.

2 Statistics will prove anything, even the truth.

Noël Moynihan (1916–94)
British doctor and writer.
Attrib.

3 A single death is a tragedy; a million is a statistic.

Joseph Stalin (J. Dzhugashvili; 1879–1953)
Soviet statesman.

STUPIDITY

1 His mind is open; yes, it is so open that nothing is retained; ideas simply pass through him.

F. H. Bradley (1846–1924)
British philosopher.
Attrib.

2 You've got the brain of a four-year-old boy, and I bet he was glad to get rid of it.

Groucho Marx (Julius Marx; 1895–1977)
US comedian.

SUCCESS

1 The penalty of success is to be bored by people who used to snub you.

Nancy Astor (1879–1964)
American-born British politician.

2 The shortest and best way to make your fortune is to let people see clearly that it is in their interests to promote yours.

Jean de La Bruyère (1645–96)
French satirist.

3 When you reach the top, that's when the climb begins.

Michael Caine (1933–)
British actor.

4 The reward of a thing well done is to have done it.

Ralph Waldo Emerson (1803–82)
US poet and essayist.

5 The only place where success comes before work is a dictionary.

Vidal Sassoon (1928–)
British hair stylist.

6   There are no gains without pains.

Adlai Stevenson (1900–65)
US statesman.

SUPERSTITION

1   Of course I don't believe in it. But I understand that it brings you luck whether you believe in it or not.

Niels Bohr (1885–1962)
Danish physicist.
When asked why he had a horseshoe on his wall

2   I am a great believer in luck, and I find the harder I work the more I have of it.

Stephen Leacock (1869–1944)
English-born Canadian economist and humorist.

SUPPORT

1   What I want is men who will support me when I am in the wrong.

Lord Melbourne (1779–1848)
British statesman.
Replying to someone who said he would support Melbourne as long as he was in the right

SURVIVAL

1   I haven't asked you to make me young again. All I want is to go on getting older.

Konrad Adenauer (1876–1967)
German statesman.
Replying to his doctor

TALENT

1 The English instinctively admire any man who has no talent and is modest about it.

James Agate (1877–1947)
British theatre critic.
Attrib.

2 Whom the gods wish to destroy they first call promising.

Cyril Connolly (1903–74)
British journalist.

TAXATION

1 Sir, I now pay you this exorbitant charge, but I must ask you to explain to her Majesty that she must not in future look upon me as a source of income.

Charles Kemble (1775–1854)
British actor.
On being obliged to hand over his income tax to the tax collector

TECHNOLOGY

1 What is the use of a new-born child?

Benjamin Franklin (1706–90)
US scientist and statesman.
Response when asked the same question of a new
invention

2 One machine can do the work of fifty ordinary men. No machine can do the work of one extraordinary man.

Elbert Hubbard (1856–1915)
US writer.

TEMPTATION

1   I never resist temptation because I have found that things that are bad for me never tempt me.

George Bernard Shaw (1856–1950)
Irish dramatist and critic.

2   The only way to get rid of a temptation is to yield to it.

Oscar Wilde (1854–1900)
Irish-born British dramatist.
Repeating a similar sentiment expressed by Clementina Stirling Graham (1782–1877)

THEATRE

1   You know, I go to the theatre to be entertained…I don't want to see plays about rape, sodomy and drug addiction…I can get all that at home.

Peter Cook (1937–95)
British writer and entertainer.

THEORY

1   Dear friend, theory is all grey,
And the golden tree of life is green.

Goethe (1749–1832)
German poet and dramatist.

2   It is a good morning exercise for a research scientist to discard a pet hypothesis every day before breakfast. It keeps him young.

Konrad Lorenz (1903–89)
Austrian zoologist.

THINKING

1 The most fluent talkers or most plausible reasoners are not always the justest thinkers.

William Hazlitt (1778–1830)
British essayist.

2 You can't think rationally on an empty stomach, and a whole lot of people can't do it on a full one either.

Lord Reith (1889–1971)
British administrator.

3 Many people would sooner die than think. In fact they do.

Bertrand Russell (1872–1970)
British philosopher.

TIME

1 The Future is something which everyone reaches at the rate of sixty minutes an hour, whatever he does, whoever he is.

C. S. Lewis (1898–1963)
British academic and writer.

2 Time is what prevents everything from happening at once.

John Archibald Wheeler (1911–)
US theoretical physicist.

TOLERANCE

1 It is flattering some men to endure them.

Lord Halifax (1633–95)
English statesman.

2   If you cannot mould yourself as you would wish, how can
    you expect other people to be entirely to your liking?

Thomas à Kempis
German monk.

3   Steven's mind was so tolerant that he could have attended
    a lynching every day without becoming critical.

Thorne Smith (1892–1934)
US humorist.

TRAVEL

1   The time to enjoy a European tour is about three weeks
    after you unpack.

George Ade (1866–1944)
US dramatist and humorist.

2   My experience of ships is that on them one makes an
    interesting discovery about the world. One finds one can
    do without it completely.

Malcolm Bradbury (1932–)
British novelist.

TRUST

1   We are inclined to believe those whom we do not know
    because they have never deceived us.

Samuel Johnson (1709–84)
British lexicographer.

TRUTH

1   The truth that makes men free is for the most part the truth which men prefer not to hear.

Herbert Sebastian Agar (1897–1980)
US writer.

2   And ye shall know the truth, and the truth shall make you free.

Bible: John

3   Some men love truth so much that they seem to be in continual fear lest she should catch a cold on overexposure.

Samuel Butler (1835–1902)
British writer.

4   It is an old maxim of mine that when you have excluded the impossible, whatever remains, however improbable, must be the truth.

Arthur Conan Doyle (1856–1930)
British writer.

5   Truth, like a torch, the more it's shook it shines.

William Hamilton (1788–1856)
Scottish philosopher.

6   There are no new truths, but only truths that have not been recognized by those who have perceived them without noticing.

Mary McCarthy (1912–89)
US novelist.

7   It takes two to speak the truth – one to speak, and another to hear.

Henry David Thoreau (1817–62)
US writer.

UNCERTAINTY

1   Of course not. After all, I may be wrong.

Bertrand Russell (1872–1970)
British philosopher.
On being asked whether he would be prepared to die for his beliefs

UNDERSTANDING

1   Only one man ever understood me…And he didn't
understand me.

G. W. F. Hegel (1770–1831)
German philosopher.
Said on his deathbed

2   I used to tell my husband that, if he could make *me*
understand something, it would be clear to all the other
people in the country.

Eleanor Roosevelt (1884–1962)
US writer and lecturer.

UNIVERSE

1   I am very interested in the Universe – I am specializing in
the Universe and all that surrounds it.

Peter Cook (1937–95)
British writer and entertainer.

2   Had I been present at the Creation, I would have given
some useful hints for the better ordering of the universe.

Alfonso the Wise (c. 1221–84)
King of Castile and Léon.
Referring to the complicated Ptolemaic model of the universe. Often quoted as, 'Had I been consulted I would have recommended something simpler'.

VERBOSITY

1 I have made this letter longer than usual, only because I have not had the time to make it shorter.

Blaise Pascal (1623–62)
French philosopher and mathematician.

VICE

1 Vice is its own reward.

Quentin Crisp (c. 1910–99)
British model, publicist, and writer.

2 Whenever I'm caught between two evils, I take the one I've never tried.

Mae West (1892–1980)
US actress.

VICTORY

1 It was easier to conquer it than to know what to do with it.

Horace Walpole (1717–97)
British writer.
Referring to the East

2 I always say that, next to a battle lost, the greatest misery is a battle gained.

Duke of Wellington (1769–1852)
British general and statesman.

VIOLENCE

1 Violence is the repartee of the illiterate.

Alan Brien (1925–)
British journalist.

2 Nothing is ever done in this world until men are prepared to kill each other if it is not done.

George Bernard Shaw (1856–1950)
Irish dramatist and critic.

VIRTUE

1 To be able to practise five things everywhere under heaven constitutes perfect virtue…gravity, generosity of soul, sincerity, earnestness, and kindness.

Confucius (K'ung Fu-tzu; 551–479 BC)
Chinese philosopher.

2 Woman's virtue is man's greatest invention.

Cornelia Otis Skinner (1901–79)
US stage actress.
Attrib.

WALES

1 The land of my fathers. My fathers can have it.

Dylan Thomas (1914–53)
Welsh poet.

2 There are still parts of Wales where the only concession to gaiety is a striped shroud.

Gwyn Thomas (1913–81)
British writer.

WAR

1 It takes twenty years or more of peace to make a man, it takes only twenty seconds of war to destroy him.

Baudouin I (1930–93)
King of Belgium.

2 My centre is giving way, my right is in retreat; situation excellent. I shall attack.

Marshal Foch (1851–1929)
French soldier.
Message sent during the second Battle of the Marne, 1918.

3 If sunbeams were weapons of war, we would have had solar energy long ago.

George Porter (1920–)
British chemist.

4 As long as war is regarded as wicked, it will always have its fascination. When it is looked upon as vulgar, it will cease to be popular.

Oscar Wilde (1854–1900)
Irish-born British dramatist.

WEAPONS

1 It was very successful, but it fell on the wrong planet.

Wernher von Braun (1912–77)
German rocket engineer.
Referring to the first V2 rocket to hit London during World War II

WEDDINGS

1   If it were not for the presents, an elopement would be preferable.

George Ade (1866–1944)
US dramatist and humorist.

2   It is a truth universally acknowledged, that a single man in possession of a good fortune must be in want of a wife.

Jane Austen (1775–1817)
British novelist.
The opening words of *Pride and Prejudice*

3   Wives are young men's mistresses, companions for middle age, and old men's nurses.

Francis Bacon (1561–1626)
English philosopher.

4   He was reputed one of the wise men, that made answer to the question, when a man should marry? A young man not yet, an elder man not at all.

Francis Bacon

5   It is easier to be a lover than a husband, for the same reason that it is more difficult to show a ready wit all day long than to produce an occasional *bon mot*.

Honoré de Balzac (1799–1850)
French novelist.

6   Let the husband render unto the wife due benevolence: and likewise also the wife unto the husband.

Bible: I Corinthians

7   But if they cannot contain, let them marry: for it is better to marry than to burn.

Bible: I Corinthians

8   Ah, gentle dames! It gars me greet
To think how mony counsels sweet,
How mony lengthen'd sage advices,
The husband frae the wife despises!

Robert Burns (1759–96)
Scottish poet.

9   An archaeologist is the best husband any woman can have: the older she gets, the more interested he is in her.

Agatha Christie (1891–1976)
British detective-story writer.

10   Marriage is a wonderful invention; but then again so is a bicycle repair kit.

Billy Connolly (1942–)
British comedian.

11   Husbands are like fires. They go out when unattended.

Zsa Zsa Gabor (1919–)
Hungarian-born US film star.

12   The concept of two people living together for 25 years without having a cross word suggests a lack of spirit only to be admired in sheep.

A. P. Herbert (1890–1971)
British writer and politican.

13   The triumph of hope over experience.

Samuel Johnson (1709–84)
British lexicographer.
Referring to the hasty remarriage of an acquaintance following the death of his first wife, with whom he had been most unhappy

14 Love is moral even without legal marriage, but marriage is immoral without love.

Ellen Key (Karolina Sofia Key; 1849–1926)
Swedish writer.

15 It has been said that a bride's attitude towards her betrothed can be summed up in three words: Aisle. Altar. Hymn.

Frank Muir (1920–98)
British writer and broadcaster.

16 Strange to say what delight we married people have to see these poor fools decoyed into our condition.

Samuel Pepys (1633–1703)
English diarist.

17 It doesn't much signify whom one marries, for one is sure to find next morning that it was someone else.

Samuel Rogers (1763–1855)
British poet.

18 Never trust a husband too far, nor a bachelor too near.

Helen Rowland (1876–1950)
US writer.

19 It takes two to make a marriage a success and only one a failure.

Herbert Samuel (1870–1963)
British Liberal statesman.

20 Marriage is popular because it combines the maximum of temptation with the maximum of opportunity.

George Bernard Shaw (1856–1950)
Irish dramatist and critic.

21 Remember, it is as easy to marry a rich woman as a poor woman.

William Makepeace Thackeray (1811–63)
British novelist.

22 Marriage is the only adventure open to the cowardly.

Voltaire (François-Marie Arouet; 1694–1778)
French writer.

23 LORD ILLINGWORTH. The Book of Life begins with a man and a woman in a garden.
MRS ALLONBY. It ends with Revelations.

Oscar Wilde (1854–1900)
Irish-born British dramatist.

24 A man looks pretty small at a wedding, George. All those good women standing shoulder to shoulder, making sure that the knot's tied in a mighty public way.

Thornton Wilder (1897–1975)
US novelist and dramatist.

WISDOM

1 For in much wisdom is much grief: and he that increaseth knowledge increaseth sorrow.

Bible: Ecclesiastes

2 Be wiser than other people if you can, but do not tell them so.

Earl of Chesterfield (1694–1773)
English statesman.

3 It is the province of knowledge to speak and it is the privilege of wisdom to listen.

Oliver Wendell Holmes (1809–94)
US writer.

WOMEN

1   A woman seldom asks advice until she has bought her wedding clothes.

   Joseph Addison (1672–1719)
   British essayist.

2   One is not born a woman, one becomes one.

   Simone de Beauvoir (1908–86)
   French writer.

3   Most women are not so young as they are painted.

   Max Beerbohm (1872–1956)
   British writer.

4   Brigands demand your money or your life; women require both.

   Samuel Butler (1835–1902)
   British writer.

5   Wherever one wants to be kissed.

   Coco Chanel (1883–1971)
   French dress designer.
   When asked where one should wear perfume

6   I should like to know what is the proper function of women, if it is not to make reasons for husbands to stay at home, and still stronger reasons for bachelors to go out.

   George Eliot (Mary Ann Evans; 1819–80)
   British novelist.

7   When a woman behaves like a man, why doesn't she behave like a nice man?

Edith Evans (1888–1976)
British actress.

8 My mother said it was simple to keep a man, you must be a maid in the living room, a cook in the kitchen and a whore in the bedroom. I said I'd hire the other two and take care of the bedroom bit.

Jerry Hall (1956–)
US model and actress.

9 I expect that Woman will be the last thing civilized by Man.

George Meredith (1828–1909)
British novelist.

10 One tongue is sufficient for a woman.

John Milton (1608–74)
English poet.
On being asked whether he would allow his daughters to learn foreign languages

11 Scarce, sir. Mighty scarce.

Mark Twain (Samuel Langhorne Clemens; 1835–1910)
US writer.
Responding to the question 'In a world without women what would men become?'

12 Once a woman has given you her heart you can never get rid of the rest of her.

John Vanbrugh

13 Women have served all these centuries as looking-glasses possessing the magic and delicious power of reflecting the figure of man at twice its natural size.

Virginia Woolf (1882–1941)
British novelist.

WORK

1   One cubic foot less of space and it would have constituted adultery.

Robert Benchley (1889–1945)
US humorist.
Describing an office shared with Dorothy Parker

2   Whatsoever thy hand findeth to do, do it with thy might; for there is no work, nor device, nor knowledge, nor wisdom, in the grave, whither thou goest.

Bible: Ecclesiastes

3   Work is the grand cure of all the maladies and miseries that ever beset mankind.

Thomas Carlyle (1795–1881)
Scottish historian and essayist.

4   Industrial relations are like sexual relations. It's better between two consenting parties.

Vic Feather (1908–76)
British trade-union leader.

5   By working faithfully eight hours a day you may eventually get to be a boss and work twelve hours a day.

Robert Frost (1875–1963)
US poet.

6   The way to get things done is not to mind who gets the credit of doing them.

Benjamin Jowett (1817–93)
British theologian.

7   Happy is the man with a wife to tell him what to do and a secretary to do it.

Lord Mancroft (1917–87)
British businessman and writer.

8   Be nice to people on your way up because you'll meet 'em on your way down.

Wilson Mizner (1876–1933)
US writer and wit.
Also attributed to Jimmy Durante

9   They say hard work never hurt anybody, but I figure why take the chance.

Ronald Reagan (1911–)
US Republican president.

10   One of the symptoms of approaching nervous breakdown is the belief that one's work is terribly important.

Bertrand Russell (1872–1970)
British philosopher.

11   It might be said that it is the ideal of the employer to have production without employees and the ideal of the employee is to have income without work.

E. F. Schumacher (1911–77)
German-born economist.

12   Work is the curse of the drinking classes.

Oscar Wilde (1854–1900)
Irish-born British dramatist.

13   If two men on the same job agree all the time, then one is useless. If they disagree all the time, then both are useless.

Darryl F. Zanuck (1902–79)
US film producer.

WORRY

1 When I look back on all these worries I remember the story of the old man who said on his deathbed that he had had a lot of trouble in his life, most of which had never happened.

Winston Churchill (1874–1965)
British statesman.

2 I have never known a man who died from overwork, but many who died from doubt.

Charles H. Mayo (1865–1939)
US physician.

YOUTH

1 Youth is something very new: twenty years ago no one mentioned it.

Coco Chanel (1883–1971)
French dress designer.

2 The young always have the same problem – how to rebel and conform at the same time. They have now solved this by defying their parents and copying one another.

Quentin Crisp (c. 1910– 99)
Model, publicist, and writer.

3 Oh, I was so much older then, I'm younger than that now.

Bob Dylan (Robert Zimmerman; 1941–)
US singer and songwriter.

4 Youth will come here and beat on my door, and force its way in.

Henrik Ibsen (1828–1906)
Norwegian dramatist.

5 Towering in the confidence of twenty-one.

Samuel Johnson (1709–84)
British lexicographer.

6 The atrocious crime of being a young man...I shall neither attempt to palliate nor deny.

William Pitt the Elder (1708–78)
British statesman.

7 My salad days,
When I was green in judgment, cold in blood,
To say as I said then!

William Shakespeare (1564–1616)
English dramatist and critic.

8 Live as long as you may, the first twenty years are the longest half of your life.

Robert Southey (1774–1843)
British poet.

KEYWORD INDEX

A

abomination A lie is an a.   LYING, 2

abroad an honest man sent to lie a. for…his country   DIPLOMACY, 5

absence A. is to love   LEAVING, 4

accelerator You just press the a. to the floor and steer left   SPORT, 12

ace someone else was about to play the a.   CRITICISM, 2

achieved Nothing great was ever a.   ENTHUSIASM, 1

acquaintance hope our a. may be a long 'un   SPEECHES, 3

act character actor is one who cannot a.   OCCUPATIONS, 11

acting A. is the most minor of gifts   OCCUPATIONS, 6

the art of a. is not to act   OCCUPATIONS, 7

actor a. is something less than a man   OCCUPATIONS, 2

a.…reminds you of an animal   OCCUPATIONS, 12

Every a. in his heart   OCCUPATIONS, 13

great a.…lousy husband   OCCUPATIONS, 4

greatest love affairs…involved one a.   OCCUPATIONS, 9

Scratch an a.…find an actress   OCCUPATIONS, 10

When an a. has money   OCCUPATIONS, 3

actors patience with the jealousies…of a.   OCCUPATIONS, 5

pick out a. by the glazed look   OCCUPATIONS, 14

actress an a. to be a success   OCCUPATIONS, 1

great a.…the devil   OCCUPATIONS, 4

actresses A. will happen   OCCUPATIONS, 8

addictive sin tends to be a.   SIN, 1

admiring the cure for a. the House of Lords   HOUSES OF PARLIAMENT, 2

adolescence maturity is only a short break in a.   AGE, 9

adores he a. his maker   CONCEIT, 3

adultery commit a. at one end   ADULTERY, 2

the Tasmanians, who never committed a.   ADULTERY, 4

would have constituted a.   WORK, 1

advantage The a. of doing one's praising   PRAISE, 2

adventure Marriage is the only a. open to the cowardly   WEDDINGS, 21

advice A. is seldom welcome   ADVICE, 1

intended to give you some a.   ADVICE, 2

woman seldom asks a.   WOMEN, 1

yet to hear…earnest a. from my seniors   ADVICE, 4

against not a. the police   OCCUPATIONS, 90

age A. cannot wither her   COMPLIMENTS, 3

a. finds out was dew   AGE, 3

I prefer old a. to the alternative   AGE, 5

aged a. diplomats   DIPLOMACY, 1

agenda Our a. is now exhausted   AGREEMENT, 3

aging A.…the only…way to live a long time   AGE, 1

agree a. to a thing in principle   AGREEMENT, 1

don't say you a. with me   AGREEMENT, 4

If two men on the same job a.   WORK, 13

agreement My people and I have come to an a.   FREEDOM, 1

ain't bet you a hundred bucks he a. in here   FUNERALS, 3

airplane The a. stays up because it doesn't have the time to fall   SCIENCE, 5

aisle A.. Altar. Hymn   WEDDINGS, 15

alcohol A.…enables Parliament to do things at eleven   DRINKING, 15

A. is like love   DRINKING, 5

alive not one will still be a. in a hundred years' time   MORTALITY, 7

all a man, take him for a. in a.   COMPLIMENTS, 4

altar Aisle. A.. Hymn   WEDDINGS, 15

alternative prefer old age to the a.   AGE, 5

amateur the last time that I will take part as an a.   FUNERALS, 1

amplified I'm being a. by the mike   SPEECHES, 2

amuse cherish our friends not for their ability to a. us   FRIENDSHIP, 12

ancestors when his half-civilized a. were hunting the wild boar   JEWS, 1

anecdotage man fell into his a.   AGE, 7

angel In heaven an a. is nobody in particular   EQUALITY, 4

angels A. can fly   SERIOUSNESS, 1

animal Man is the only a.…terms with the victims…he eats   HYPOCRISY, 1

This a. is very bad   SELF-PRESERVATION, 1

Whenever you observe an an. closely   ANIMALS, 2

animals a.…know nothing…of what people say about them   ANIMALS, 5

But if we stop loving a.   ANIMALS, 5

There are two things for which a. are…envied   ANIMALS, 6

another I would have given you a.   CHIVALRY, 2

answer give a. as need requireth   EDUCATION, 1

wisest man can a.   EDUCATION, 4

ants closer to the a. than the butterflies   LEISURE, 1

anybody don't have to respect a.   AGE, 4

who you are, you aren't a.   FAME, 4

anyone a. here whom I have not insulted   SPEECHES, 25

apologize a good rule in life never to a.   APOLOGIES, 3

apparatus *Brain*, n. An a. with which we think   EDUCATION, 2

applause I want to thank you for stopping the
a.   SPEECHES, 5
appreciation looks back with a. to the brilliant
teachers   OCCUPATIONS, 128
Arabs The Jews and A. should…settle their
differences   RELIGION, 1
archaeologist An a. is the best husband
                                                    WEDDINGS, 9
archbishop the sign of an a. is a double-cross
                                                OCCUPATIONS, 35
architect physician can bury his mistakes, but
the a.   MISTAKES, 3
arguments A. are to be avoided
                                                  ARGUMENTS, 6
aristocracy a.…government by the badly
educated   DEMOCRACY, 2
arm Don't carry away that a. till I have…my
ring   PRACTICALITY, 1
arm'd a. with more than complete steel
                                                    JUSTICE, 1
army If you don't want to use the a., I should
like to borrow it   SARCASM, 1
arrest My father didn't create you to a. me
                                                OCCUPATIONS, 92
arrow Every a.…feels the attraction of earth
                                                   AMBITION, 2
art a. of looking for trouble
                                                OCCUPATIONS, 44
Modern a. is what happens
                                                OCCUPATIONS, 15
Mr Goldwyn…you are only interested in a.
                                                      ART, 6
artist a. must know how to convince
                                                OCCUPATIONS, 22
a.…produces things that people don't need
                                                OCCUPATIONS, 24
a. who always paints the same scene pleases
the public   OCCUPATIONS, 23
believe only what an a. does
                                                OCCUPATIONS, 18
artists A.…they live mainly in the red
                                                OCCUPATIONS, 20
ask To labour and not a. for any reward
                                               SELFLESSNESS, 1
aspect Meet in her a.   COMPLIMENTS, 1
aspirations The young have a.   AGE, 19
ass average schoolmaster is…essentially an a.
                                                OCCUPATIONS, 130
astonish gratify some people, and a. the rest
                                                      RIGHT, 2
attack I shall a.   WAR, 2
love until after the first a.   LOVE, 4
attention take his a. away from the universe
                                                     PRAYER, 1
attraction Every arrow…feels the a. of earth
                                                   AMBITION, 2
audience enjoy appearing before a British a.
                                                   SPEECHES, 26
the a. was a disaster   SPEECHES, 29
Australia he was born in A.   PLACES, 9
author As if a man were a. of himself
                                               SELF-RELIANCE, 2
a. is a man of genius   OCCUPATIONS, 28
a. who speaks about his own books
                                                OCCUPATIONS, 26

dangerous to an a. as silence
                                                OCCUPATIONS, 29
authority No morality can be founded on a.
                                                    MORALITY, 2
teacher should have maximal a.
                                                OCCUPATIONS, 133
authors A. are easy to get on with
                                                OCCUPATIONS, 31

B

babies If men had to have b.   CHILDREN, 4
baby Every b. born into the world
                                                    CHILDREN, 5
bachelor Never trust…a b. too near
                                                    WEDDINGS, 18
bachelors reasons for b. to go out
                                                      WOMEN, 6
back any of you at the b. who do not hear me
                                                    SPEECHES, 1
bad she was a very b. cook   SNOBBERY, 3
when I'm b. I'm better   SEX, 13
bald being b. – one can hear snowflakes
                                                 APPEARANCE, 2
ball Casting a b. at three straight sticks
                                                      SPORT, 5
banality b. of evil   EVIL, 1
bandits Critics!…Those cut-throat b.
                                                OCCUPATIONS, 33
bands Brass b. are all very well in their place
                                                      MUSIC, 2
banned any book should be b.
                                                  CENSORSHIP, 4
barbarism gone directly from b. to
degeneration   AMERICA, 1
bargains rule for b.   BUSINESS, 2
based All progress is b.   PROGRESS, 2
bat They came to see me b. not to see you
bowl   SPORT, 3
bathroom goes to church as he goes to the b.
                                                    RELIGION, 3
battalions God is always on the side of the big
b.   POWER, 2
God is on the side not of the heavy b.
                                                      POWER, 9
battle greatest misery is a b. gained
                                                    VICTORY, 4
into b. sitting down   OCCUPATIONS, 119
bear-baiting Puritan hated b.   MORALITY, 5
beautiful most b. things…are the most
useless   BEAUTY, 4
beauty A thing of b. is a joy for ever
                                                     BEAUTY, 1
b. is only sin deep   BEAUTY, 5
B. is truth, truth b.   BEAUTY, 2
b. of a thousand stars   BEAUTY, 3
She walks in b.   COMPLIMENTS, 1
The pain passes, but the b. remains
                                                  ENDURANCE, 3
because B. it is there   ACHIEVEMENT, 3
bed Never go to b. mad   ARGUMENTS, 2
bedroom whore in the b.   WOMEN, 8
beg only the poor…are forbidden to b.
                                                    POVERTY, 2
begin B. low, speak slow
                                                    SPEECHES, 7

when the guns b. to shoot
OCCUPATIONS, 115

begins everything b. somewhere
BEGINNINGS, 2

belief the b. that one's work is…important
WORK, 10

believe don't b. in…true love until after the
first attack LOVE, 4

inclined to b. those whom we do not know
TRUST, 1

it brings you luck whether you b.…or not
SUPERSTITION, 1

you must b. in God FAITH, 2

benefactors gratitude to most b. is the same
as…for dentists INGRATITUDE, 1

benevolence husband render unto the wife
due b. WEDDINGS, 6

best all that's b. of dark and bright
COMPLIMENTS, 1

we live in the b. of all possible worlds
OPTIMISM, 1

betray All a man can b. CONSCIENCE, 1

betraying to choose between b. my country
and b. my friend BETRAYAL, 1

betrothed a bride's attitude towards her b.
WEDDINGS, 15

better b. to marry than to burn
WEDDINGS, 7

when I'm bad I'm b. SEX, 13

Bibles they have the land and we have the B.
RELIGION, 6

big If you're not b. enough to lose
DEFEAT, 3

biography history…is but the b. of great men
GREATNESS, 1

bigamy B. is having one wife too many
MARRIAGE, 1

bird-cage a b. played with toasting-forks
MUSIC, 4

Robert Houdin who…invented the vanishing
b. trick SPEECHES, 28

birth From b. to age eighteen, a girl needs
good parents AGE, 25

birthday A diplomat…always remembers a
woman's b. AGE, 11

bishop blonde to make a b. kick a hole
APPEARANCE, 1

How can a b. marry OCCUPATIONS, 36

the symbol of a b. is a crook
OCCUPATIONS, 35

blank Where were you fellows when the paper
was b. OCCUPATIONS, 58

block there's a statue inside every b. of stone
OBESITY, 3

blockhead b. ever wrote except for money
OCCUPATIONS, 30

blonde A b. to make a bishop kick a hole
APPEARANCE, 1

bloom It's a sort of b. on a woman
CHARM, 1

blush b. to find it fame GOOD, 4

boar when his half-civilized ancestors were
hunting the wild b. JEWS, 1

bon to produce an occasional *b. mot*
WEDDINGS, 5

book A b. may be amusing BOOKS, 4

any b. should be banned CENSORSHIP, 4

go away and write a b. about it
SPEECHES, 10

The number one b.…was written by a
committee BUREAUCRACY, 4

What you don't know would make a great b.
IGNORANCE, 2

books author who speaks about his own b.
OCCUPATIONS, 21

b. by which the printers have lost
BOOKS, 3

of making many b. there is no end
BOOKS, 1

Whenever b. are burned CENSORSHIP, 2

bookseller he once shot a b.
OCCUPATIONS, 34

boon Is life a b. MORTALITY, 4

boots before the truth has got its b. on
LYING, 1

Very well, then I shall not take off my b.
PRACTICALITY, 2

bordello After I die, I shall return to earth as a
gatekeeper of a b. MUSIC, 8

bore *B.,* n. A person who talks SPEECH, 1

when you b. people, they think it's their fault
FAME, 3

bored aged diplomats to be b.
DIPLOMACY, 1

Punctuality is the virtue of the b.
PROMPTNESS, 1

We were as nearly b. as enthusiasm would
permit CRITICISM, 4

When you're b. with yourself, marry
MARRIAGE, 9

boredom The effect of b.…in history
BOREDOM, 2

born b. to obey LEADERSHIP, 1

joy that a man is b. into the world
CHILDREN, 2

borrow If you don't want to use the army, I
should like to b. it SARCASM, 1

boss working…eight hours a day…get to be a
b. WORK, 5

both man who sees b. sides…sees absolutely
nothing NONCOMMITMENT, 3

bottles It is with…people as with…b.
CHARACTER, 1

the English have hot-water b. ENGLAND, 6

bowl They came to see me bat not to see you
b. SPORT, 3

boy rarely…one can see in a little b. the
promise of a man CHILDREN, 6

boys B. do not grow up gradually
CHILDREN, 3

Where…b. plan for what…young girls plan
for whom MEN AND WOMEN, 11

brain *B.,* n. An apparatus with which we think
EDUCATION, 2

b. of a four-year-old boy
STUPIDITY, 2

important messages from the b.
SPEECHES, 12

the human b. is a device to keep the ears
from grating EDUCATION, 5

brains What good are b. to a man
INTELLECT, 7

brass B. bands are all very well in their place
MUSIC, 2

brave we could never learn to be b....if there
were only joy ENDURANCE, 1

bread b. and circuses PUBLIC, 6
Their learning is like b. in a besieged town
SCOTLAND, 3

breakfast b.... I told Jeeves to drink it himself
DRINKING, 17

breeding Good b. consists in concealing
how...we think of ourselves MANNERS, 2

brevity B. is the soul of lingerie
CLOTHES, 3
B. is the soul of wit SPEECHES, 21

bride a b.'s attitude towards her betrothed
WEDDINGS, 15

bridge over the B. of Sighs into eternity
DEATH, 7

brief Be sincere, be b., be seated
SPEECHES, 20

brigands B. demand your money
WOMEN, 4

brilliant a far less b. pen than mine
BOASTS, 1

bring thou knowest not what a day may b.
forth FUTURE, 1

brothel b. for the emotions
SENTIMENTALITY, 1

brotherly let b. love continue
HOSPITALITY, 1

buck The b. stops here RESPONSIBILITY, 3

bucks bet you a hundred b. he ain't in here
FUNERALS, 4

buds the darling b. of May COMPLIMENTS, 5

building twenty years of marriage make her...
like a public b. MARRIAGE, 15

bull Better send them a Papal B.
MISTAKES, 1
When you take the b. by the horns...
CHANCE, 1

burn better to marry than to b.
WEDDINGS, 7

burned Whenever books are b.
CENSORSHIP, 2

burning To keep a lamp b. CHARITY, 3

business A b. that makes nothing but money
BUSINESS, 3
b. sagacity reduces itself BUSINESS, 12
B. underlies everything in our national life
BUSINESS, 14

bust funny thing about that b. AGE, 22

butter b. wouldn't melt in her mouth
INSULTS, 1

butterflies closer to the ants than the b.
LEISURE, 1

butterfly Happiness is like a b.
HAPPINESS, 2

C

Caesar C.'s wife PURITY, 3

cake The art of dividing a c. DIPLOMACY, 4

calamities C. are of two kinds
MISFORTUNE, 1

calf but the c. won't get much sleep
MISTRUST, 1

cancel to c. half a Line DESTINY, 1

candle little c. throws his beams GOOD, 5

candles She would rather light c. than curse
the darkness COMPLIMENTS, 7

capitalism C. is the exploitation of man
COMMUNISM, 1

cards sorry I have not learned to play
at c. GAMES, 5
wonderful to see persons of the best sense...
shuffling and dividing a pack of c. GAMES, 1

catastrophe When a man confronts c....a
woman looks in her mirror
MEN AND WOMEN, 10

cathedral One c. is worth a hundred
theologians RELIGION, 2

Catherine I'm glad you like my C. SEX, 11

cause A c. is like champagne BELIEF, 1

celebrity A c....works hard...to become
known FAME, 1
The nice thing about being a c. FAME, 3

celery Genuineness...Like c. SINCERITY, 2

censorship C....depraving and corrupting
CENSORSHIP, 3

centre My c. is giving way WAR, 2

chaff An editor...separates the wheat from the
c. OCCUPATIONS, 61

chambermaid as happy in the arms of a c.
IMAGINATION, 1

champagne A cause is like c. BELIEF, 1
like a glass of c. that has stood
HOUSES OF PARLIAMENT, 1
water flowed like c. ABSTINENCE, 4

Charing-Cross the full tide of human existence
is at C. LONDON, 1

Chartreuse religious system that produced
green C. DRINKING, 13

chastity c. is no more a virtue than
malnutrition ABSTINENCE, 2
Give me c. and continence MORALITY, 1

cheating Peace...a period of c. PEACE, 1

chess Life's too short for c. GAMES, 2
victim of c. GAMES, 3

child c. of five would understand this
SIMPLICITY, 1
What is the use of a new-born c.
TECHNOLOGY, 1
wise father that knows his own c.
FAMILY, 7

childbirth Death and taxes and c.
CHILDREN, 9

children C. have never been very good at
listening CHILDREN, 1
He that has no c. CHILDREN, 11
Never have c. CHILDREN, 14
Parents...a disappointment to their c.
CHILDREN, 6
Parents learn a lot from their c.
CHILDREN, 13

Chopin to bridge the awful gap between
Dorothy and C. MUSIC, 1

Christ If Jesus C. were to come to-day
BELIEF, 3
only a male can represent C. RELIGION, 4

Christianity C.,...but why journalism
OCCUPATIONS, 65
decay of C. DRINKING, 13
Christians settle their differences like good C.
RELIGION, 1
church goes to c. as he goes to the bathroom
RELIGION, 3
circumcised When they c. Herbert Samuel
INSULTS, 3
circuses bread and c. PUBLIC, 6
city that unnatural c. where everyone is an
exile AMERICA, 3
It is a c. where you can see a sparrow fall
IRELAND, 5
civilized c. man cannot live without cooks
OCCUPATIONS, 38
Woman will be the last thing c. by Man
WOMEN, 9
clean hard to be funny when you have to be c.
HUMOUR, 3
clear His right was c., his will was strong
RIGHT, 1
if he could make *me* understand...it would be
c. to all UNDERSTANDING, 2
clenched You cannot shake hands with a c.
fist COMPROMISE, 1
clever not c. but...always right
SELF-CONFIDENCE, 1
too c. to understand PREJUDICE, 1
climb Fain would I c., yet fear I to fall
AMBITION, 3
climbing c. is performed in the same position
with creeping AMBITION, 4
clock colleagues generally present him with a
c. LEAVING, 13
clocks hands of c. in railway stations
CHILDREN, 3
pass my declining years saluting...
grandfather c. AGE, 14
stop all the c. FUNERALS, 2
close-up Life is a tragedy...in c. LIFE, 2
clothes After that you just take the girl's c. off
DRINKING, 5
bought her wedding c. WOMEN, 1
pay more for my c. CLOTHES, 1
taking off all her c. CLOTHES, 4
club I don't want to belong to any c.
HUMOUR, 6
takes you so far from the c. house
SPORT, 7
cock waiting for the c. to crow
BETRAYAL, 3
cold she should catch a c. on overexposure
TRUTH, 3
threat of a neglected c. is for doctors
OCCUPATIONS, 48
comedy Life is...a c. in long-shot LIFE, 2
command people c. rather badly
LEADERSHIP, 1
commerce honour sinks where c. long
prevails BUSINESS, 5
committee A c. is a cul-de-sac
BUREAUCRACY, 3
The number one book of the ages was written
by a c. BUREAUCRACY, 4

common theory that c. people know what they
want DEMOCRACY, 4
C. sense is the collection of prejudices
PREJUDICE, 2
common-looking The Lord prefers c. people
APPEARANCE, 5
Communism C. is like prohibition
COMMUNISM, 2
C. is the reverse COMMUNISM, 1
community journalism....keeps us in touch
with the ignorance of the c.
OCCUPATIONS, 73
Marriage...a c....making in all two
MARRIAGE, 2
companions c. for middle age
WEDDINGS, 3
company never expected justice from a c.
BUSINESS, 11
compare c. thee to a summer's day
COMPLIMENTS, 5
complaint I want to register a c.
COMPLAINTS, 1
concealing Good breeding consists in c.
how...we think of ourselves MANNERS, 2
conceit As for c. SELF-CONFIDENCE, 3
condition fools decoyed into our c.
WEDDINGS, 16
the Jews have made a contribution to the
human c. JEWS, 2
confess Men will c. HUMOUR, 2
only c. our little faults IMPERFECTION, 2
confidence c. of twenty-one YOUTH, 5
think I'm getting a little c.
SELF-CONFIDENCE, 2
conform how to rebel and c. at the same time
YOUTH, 2
conquer easier to c. it than to know what to do
VICTORY, 1
conscience C. warns us...somebody may be
looking CONSCIENCE, 2
freedom of speech, freedom of c., and the
prudence never to practise...them
FREEDOM, 8
consent No one can make you feel inferior
without your c. INFERIORITY, 1
consequences there are neither rewards nor
punishments – there are c. NATURE, 2
constant A c. guest HOSPITALITY, 2
consumer In a c. society there are...two kinds
of slaves MATERIALISM, 1
continence Give me chastity and c.
MORALITY, 1
that melancholy sexual perversion known as
c. ABSTINENCE, 6
Continent On the C. people have good food
MANNERS, 1
Continental C. people have sex life
ENGLAND, 6
contraception a terrific story about
oral c. CONTRACEPTION, 2
contraceptives C. should be used
CONTRACEPTION, 3
contradicts One often c. an opinion
ARGUMENTS, 3

conversation make his c. perfectly delightful
SPEECH, 15
Your ignorance cramps my c.
IGNORANCE, 1
conversationalist the c. who adds 'in other words'
SPEECH, 12
cook c. was a good c.
OCCUPATIONS, 40
good thing about him is his c.
OCCUPATIONS, 39
she was a very bad c.
SNOBBERY, 3
cooks civilized man cannot live without c.
OCCUPATIONS, 38
copying by defying their parents and c. one another
YOUTH, 2
corrupt Power tends to c.
POWER, 1
cost To give and not to count the c.
SELFLESSNESS, 1
count If you can...c. your money you are not...rich man
MONEY, 5
country an honest man sent to lie abroad for... his c.
DIPLOMACY, 5
our c., right or wrong
PATRIOTISM, 1
The past is a foreign c.
PAST, 3
understanding the problems of running a c.
OCCUPATIONS, 100
couple A married c. are well suited
MARRIAGE, 10
courage good deal of physical c. to ride a horse
ANIMALS, 3
courting When you are c. a nice girl
SCIENCE, 3
cowardly Marriage is the only adventure open to the c.
WEDDINGS, 21
cows daring...to explain...that c. can be eaten
RELIGION, 5
cradle Between the c. and the grave
MORTALITY, 3
create My father didn't c. you to arrest me
OCCUPATIONS, 92
Creation Had I been present at the C.
UNIVERSE, 2
credit The way to get things done is not to mind who gets the c.
WORK, 6
creditors my oldest c. would hardly know me
APPEARANCE, 3
creeds So many gods, so many c.
KINDNESS, 2
Vain are the thousand c.
BELIEF, 2
creeping climbing is performed in the same position with c.
AMBITION, 4
cricket c. as organised loafing
SPORT, 10
crime The atrocious c. of being a young man
YOUTH, 6
critic A c. is a man who
OCCUPATIONS, 46
c. is a legless man
OCCUPATIONS, 45
drama c. is a person who surprises the playwright
OCCUPATIONS, 44
ever seen a dramatic c. in the daytime
OCCUPATIONS, 47
Show me a c. without prejudices
CRITICISM, 8
critics Asking a working writer...about c.
OCCUPATIONS, 35
C.!...Those cut-throat bandits
OCCUPATIONS, 41

heaves in the presence of c.
OCCUPATIONS, 42
crook the symbol of a bishop is a c.
OCCUPATIONS, 35
cross no c., no crown
ENDURANCE, 2
crossword an optimist...fills up his c. puzzle in ink
OPTIMISM, 2
crow waiting for the cock to c.
BETRAYAL, 3
crowd a c. like that...brings a lump to my wallet
MONEY, 16
flock of sheep...a c. of men
PUBLIC, 1
crown no cross, no c.
ENDURANCE, 2
cubic One c. foot less
WORK, 1
cul-de-sac A committee is a c.
BUREAUCRACY, 3
cure the c. for admiring the House of Lords
HOUSES OF PARLIAMENT, 2
Work is the grand c.
WORK, 3
curse She would rather light candles than c. the darkness
COMPLIMENTS, 7
Work is the c. of the drinking classes
WORK, 12
curtain I saw it at a disadvantage – the c. was up
CRITICISM, 13
cushion Like a c., he always bore
INSULTS, 2
custom A c. loathsome
SMOKING, 3
c. stale /Her infinite variety
COMPLIMENTS, 3
customers When you are skinning your c.
BUSINESS, 7

D

dancers a perfectly ghastly season it's been for you Spanish d.
CHARITY, 1
dark Genuineness only thrives in the d.
SINCERITY, 2
darkness rather light candles than curse the d.
COMPLIMENTS, 7
dates Its history d. from today
ROYALTY, 2
day compare thee to a summer's d.
COMPLIMENTS, 5
I look upon every d. to be lost
FRIENDSHIP, 6
thou knowest not what a d. may bring forth
FUTURE, 1
days childish d....as long as twenty d.
NOSTALGIA, 2
d. of wine and roses
MORTALITY, 1
dead But he's just as d. as if he'd been wrong
RIGHT, 1
He was a great patriot...provided...that he really is d.
COMPLIMENTS, 9
I've just read that I am d.
OBITUARIES, 2
The past is the only d. thing
PAST, 5
dear D. 338171
HUMOUR, 5
death d. after life does greatly please
DEATH, 9
D. and taxes and childbirth
CHILDREN, 9
d....the least of all evils
DEATH, 3
D....the only thing we haven't succeeded in... vulgarizing
DEATH, 5
Football isn't...life and d.
SPORT, 9

Reports of my d. are greatly exaggerated
OBITUARIES, 3

the d. of Little Nell without laughing
INSENSITIVITY, 1

what a man still plans at the end shows the... injustice in his d.
DEATH, 4

debt A promise made is a d. unpaid
PROMISES, 2

declining pass my d. years saluting... grandfather clocks
AGE, 14

decompose d. in a barrel of porter
FUNERALS, 5

decrepit you are not yet d. enough
AGE, 8

deed good d. in a naughty world
GOOD, 5

deep beauty is only sin d.
BEAUTY, 5

defeat d. is an orphan
DEFEAT, 1

defend I disapprove of what you say, but I will d....right to say it
FREEDOM, 9

defying by d. their parents and copying one another
YOUTH, 2

delightful make his conversation perfectly d.
SPEECH, 15

delusion d. that one woman differs from another
LOVE, 7

democracy D....government by the uneducated
DEMOCRACY, 2

D. means choosing your dictators
DEMOCRACY, 3

D. means government by discussion
DEMOCRACY, 1

ills of d. can be cured by more d.
DEMOCRACY, 5

not the voting that's d.
DEMOCRACY, 6

dentist I'd sooner go to my d.
SEX, 10

dentists gratitude to most benefactors is the same as...for d.
INGRATITUDE, 1

depression Recession...a neighbour loses... d....you lose
ECONOMICS, 2

deserve I have arthritis, and I don't d. that either
AWARDS, 1

deserved I wasn't lucky. I d. it.
MERIT, 2

deserves the face he d.
AGE, 13

desire a universal innate d.
PROGRESS, 2

d. to be praised twice over
PRAISE, 3

It provokes the d.
DRINKING, 14

despise some other Englishman d. him
PLACES, 17

destination I do not think this poem will reach its d.
CRITICISM, 11

destroys d. one of the works of God we call him a sportsman
HUNTING, 3

devil the D. knows Latin
CHILDREN, 8

the world, the flesh, and the d.
OCCUPATIONS, 71

diamonds My goodness those d. are lovely
GOOD, 7

to give him d. back
MEN, 3

dictation God wrote it. I merely did his d.
ACHIEVEMENT, 6

die argue that I shall some day d.
OCCUPATIONS, 88

If a man hasn't discovered something that he would d. for
IDEALISM, 2

dies It matters not how a man d.
DEATH, 6

diet Food...part of a balanced d.
FOOD, 2

differences d. in taste or opinion are irritating
ARGUMENTS, 1

The Jews and Arabs should...settle their d.
RELIGION, 1

difficult D. do you call it, Sir
CRITICISM, 5

d. to love mankind
SELFISHNESS, 2

It is d. to be humble
HUMILITY, 1

only the first step that is d.
BEGINNING, 1

dignity added to his d. by standing on it
PRIDE, 1

dined when Thomas Jefferson d. alone
SPEECHES, 4

dinner D. at the Huntercombes'
FOOD, 3

diplomat A d....always remembers a woman's birthday
AGE, 11

A real d....can cut his neighbour's throat
DIPLOMACY, 4

d. these days...a head-waiter
DIPLOMACY, 5

diplomats aged d. to be bored
DIPLOMACY, 1

disapprove I d. of what you say, but I will defend...your right to say it
FREEDOM, 9

disaster the audience was a d.
SPEECHES, 29

discoveries None of the great d.
DISCOVERY, 1

discovery D. consists of seeing what everybody has seen
DISCOVERY, 2

disease d. in the family that is never mentioned
IRELAND, 7

Evil comes...like the d.; good...like the doctor
GOOD, 2

diseases Doctors...cure d. of which they know less
OCCUPATIONS, 49

disgrace a d. to our family name of Wagstaff
FAMILY, 4

dismal situation so d. that a policeman
OCCUPATIONS, 89

dissipated still keep looking so d.
DEBAUCHERY, 1

distance The d. doesn't matter
BEGINNING, 1

do I am to d. what I please
FREEDOM, 1

doctor A young d. makes a humpy graveyard
OCCUPATIONS, 54

d. found...last disorder mortal
OCCUPATIONS, 50

d. takes the fee
OCCUPATIONS, 49

Evil comes...like the disease; good...like the d.
GOOD, 2

He has been a d. a year now
OCCUPATIONS, 56

doctors D....prescribe medicines of which they know little
OCCUPATIONS, 57

D. think a lot of patients are cured
OCCUPATIONS, 51

D. will have more lives to answer for
OCCUPATIONS, 53

threat of a neglected cold is for d.
OCCUPATIONS, 48

dog A door is what a d. is...on the wrong side of
DOGS, 2

America is a large, friendly d.
AMERICA, 4

The great pleasure of a d.   DOGS, 1

dogs I loathe people who keep d.   DOGS, 3
like asking a lamp-post…about d.
    OCCUPATIONS, 43

doing Anything that is worth d.
    ORIGINALITY, 1

dollars What's a thousand d.   MONEY, 8

done The way to get things d. is not to mind
who gets the credit   WORK, 6

don't-knows One day the d. will get in
    GOVERNMENT, 1

door A d. is what a dog is…on the wrong side
of   DOGS, 2
Youth will…beat on my d.   YOUTH, 4

doormat a d. or a prostitute   FEMINISM, 2

doubt but many who died from d.
    WORRY, 2

down I started at the top and worked my way
d.   ACHIEVEMENT, 7

dreams one person who d. of making fifty
thousand pounds   LAZINESS, 3

dreamt I d. that I was making a speech
    SPEECHES, 15

dreary Dying is a very dull, d. affair
    DEATH, 8

drink d. may be said to be an equivocator with
lechery   DRINKING, 14
If I had all the money I've spent on d.
    DRINKING, 16
no one has yet found a way to d. for a living
    DRINKING, 10
One reason I don't d.   DRINKING, 2
There are five reasons we should d.
    DRINKING, 1

drinkers no verse can give pleasure…written
by d. of water   DRINKING, 6

drinking D. is the soldier's pleasure
    OCCUPATIONS, 112
resolve to give up smoking, d. and loving
    ABSTINENCE, 5
smoking cigars and…d. of alcohol
    SMOKING, 2
Work is the curse of the d. classes
    WORK, 12

driver in the d.'s seat   POWER, 2

drug Words are…the most powerful d.
    SPEECH, 11

Dublin D., though…much worse than London
    PLACES, 8

duty a stupid man…always declares that it is
his d.   EXCUSES, 3
Do your d. and leave the rest   DUTY, 1
What's a man's first d.   SINCERITY, 3

dying D. is a very dull, dreary affair
    DEATH, 8
'Tis not the d. for a faith   FAITH, 3

dykes our d.,…are ten feet deep
    BOASTS, 8

E

early E. to rise and e. to bed
    HEALTHY AND HEALTHY LIVING, 4

ears device to keep the e. from grating
    EDUCATION, 5

earth mine were princes of the e.   JEWS, 1

The meek do not inherit the e.
    HUMILITY, 2

eat E. as much as you like   OBESITY, 4

eaten daring…to explain…that cows can be e.
    RELIGION, 5

eater good e. must be a good man
    FOOD, 1

eating E.'s going to be a whole new ball game
    LEAVING, 10

eats Man is the only animal…on friendly
terms with the victims…he e.
    HYPOCRISY, 1

economist Give me a one-handed e.
    ECONOMICS, 4
slaves of some defunct e.   INFLUENCE, 3

economists All races have…e., with the
exception of the Irish   IRELAND, 1
If all e. were laid end to end   ECONOMICS, 3

editor An e.…separates the wheat from the
chaff   OCCUPATIONS, 60
e. should have a pimp for a brother
    OCCUPATIONS, 59
newspaper e. and…a fellow with a tapeworm
    OCCUPATIONS, 60

education E. is an admirable thing
    EDUCATION, 14
E. is…the soul of a society   EDUCATION, 3
E. is what survives   EDUCATION, 11
schooling interfere with my e.
    EDUCATION, 12
When a man's e. is finished   EDUCATION, 6

efficient have to be e. if you're…lazy
    LAZINESS, 1

egalitarianism The majestic e. of the law
    EQUALITY, 1

egotism e. out of its depth   SHYNESS, 1

egotist E., n. A person…more interested in
himself   CONCEIT, 2

Egyptians the E. worshipped an insect
    OCCUPATIONS, 95

eighteen From birth to age e., a girl needs
good parents   AGE, 25
she speaks e. languages. And she can't say
'No' in any of them   SEX, 9

elders miss not the discourse of the e.
    EDUCATION, 1

elopement an e. would be preferable
    WEDDINGS, 1

eloquence Talking and e. are not the same
    SPEECH, 10

else Suppose it had been someone e. who
found you like this   ADULTERY, 5

embalmer A triumph of the e.'s art
    INSULTS, 4

eminence gain great e. without ever being
right   ECONOMICS, 1

emotions brothel for the e.
    SENTIMENTALITY, 1

employed innocently e. than in getting money
    MONEY, 6

employer ideal of the e.…production without
employees   WORK, 11

employers e. wanting all sorts of servants
    OCCUPATIONS, 108

employment I will undoubtedly have to seek…gainful e.   LEAVING, 1
empty You can't think rationally on an e. stomach   THINKING, 2
end of making many books there is no e.
BOOKS, 1
Yes, to the very e.   ENDURANCE, 4
enemies do not have to forgive my e.
RUTHLESSNESS, 2
Even a paranoid can have e.   ENEMIES, 2
forgive your e.…never forget their names
ENEMIES, 1
enemy despise your e. strategically
ENEMY, 3
hasn't an e. in the world   POPULARITY, 2
It takes your e. and your friend…to hurt you
ENEMIES, 4
we must be just to our e.   OCCUPATIONS, 34
England E.…infested with people who…tell us what to do   ENGLAND, 4
E. is a paradise for women   ENGLAND, 1
E.…the envy of less happy lands
ENGLAND, 2
in E. people have good table manners
MANNERS, 1
English The baby doesn't understand E.
CHILDREN, 8
the E. have hot-water bottles   ENGLAND, 6
The E. have no respect for their language
ENGLAND, 8
The E. may not like music   MUSIC, 3
the E. take their pleasures sadly
ENGLAND, 9
the E. think of an opinion as something…to hide   ENGLAND, 3
wears them with a strong E. accent
FASHION, 2
Englishman Am I not punished enough in not being born an E.   ENGLAND, 10
An E.…forms an orderly queue of one
ENGLAND, 5
never find an E. among the underdogs
ENGLAND, 11
Remember that you are an E.   ENGLAND, 7
some other E. despise him   ENGLAND, 8
Englishmen to create Frenchmen in the image of E.   PLACES, 3
enigma a riddle wrapped in a mystery inside an e.   PLACES, 5
enjoy Certainly, there is nothing else here to e.   PARTIES, 3
e. your ice-cream while it's on your plate
PHILOSOPHY, 3
enough It comes soon e.   FUTURE, 3
enthusiasm Nothing great was ever achieved without e.   ENTHUSIASM, 1
We were as nearly bored as e. would permit
CRITICISM, 4
enthusiastic Latins are tenderly e.
PLACES, 6
envied There are two things for which animals are…e.   ANIMALS, 6
envy 2 percent moral, 48 percent indignation and 50 percent e.
MORALITY, 9

equal All men are born e. but   EQUALITY, 3
Everybody should have an e. chance
EQUALITY, 5
equally I hate everyone e.   HATE, 1
equator With the possible exception of the e.
BEGINNINGS, 2
equipping e. us with a neck   COURAGE, 2
eternal A government agency is the nearest thing to e. life   BUREAUCRACY, 5
eternity He has made his impress on e.
INFLUENCE, 1
over the Bridge of Sighs into e.   DEATH, 7
evening thou art fairer than the e. air
BEAUTY, 3
everyone I hate e. equally   HATE, 1
evidence Most men…give e. against their own understanding   SPEECH, 7
evil banality of e.   EVIL, 1
E. comes…like the disease; good…like the doctor   GOOD, 2
He who passively accepts e.   EVIL, 2
scarcely a single man…aware to know all the e. he does   EVIL, 3
evils animals…know nothing of future e.
ANIMALS, 6
death…the least of all e.   DEATH, 3
Whenever I'm caught between two e.
VICE, 2
exaggerated Reports of my death are greatly e.   OBITUARIES, 3
excess Nothing succeeds like e.
EXCESS, 2
excluded when you have e. the impossible
TRUTH, 4
executive salary of the chief e.…not a market award for achievement
BUSINESS, 5
exercise E. is bunk   SPORT, 2
get my e. acting as a pallbearer
LAZINESS, 2
exhausted Our agenda is now e.
AGREEMENT, 3
expediency e. in a long white dress
MORALITY, 3
expense one God only…the e. of two
GOD, 2
experience The triumph of hope over e.
WEDDINGS, 13
expert An e.…has made all the mistakes…in a very narrow field
EXPERTS, 1
ex-president No candidate…elected e. by such a large majority   FAILURE, 3
extinct the Tasmanians…are now e.
ADULTERY, 4
extraordinary the most e. collection of talent
SPEECHES, 4
eye A custom loathsome to the e., hateful to the nose   SMOKING, 3
less in this than meets the e.   CRITICISM, 1
man who looks you…in the e.…hiding something   INSINCERITY, 1
eyes Your e. shine like the pants
COMPLIMENTS, 2

F

face At 50, everyone has the f. he deserves
AGE, 15

I never forget a f., but   MEMORY, 1

facts F. are not science   FACTS, 1
F. are ventriloquists' dummies   FACTS, 2
f. must never get in the way of truth
OCCUPATIONS, 66

fail Others must f.   RUTHLESSNESS, 3

fairer thou art f. than the evening air
BEAUTY, 3

faith no need for any other f. than…f. in
human beings   FAITH, 1
'Tis not the dying for a f.   FAITH, 3

faithful If this man is not f. to his God
LOYALTY, 2

fall Fain would I climb, yet fear I to f.
AMBITION, 3
The airplane stays up because it doesn't have
the time to f.   SCIENCE, 5

false beware of f. prophets   DECEPTION, 1

fame blush to find it f.   GOOD, 4
book written against f.…has the author's name
on the title-page   HYPOCRISY, 2

family f. always creeps back   FAMILY, 5

farce Parliament is the longest running f.
GOVERNMENT, 3

farewells f. should be sudden   LEAVING, 5

farmer good f. is…a handy man
OCCUPATIONS, 63

farmers f., flourish and complain
OCCUPATIONS, 62

fascinates I like work; it f. me   IDLENESS, 2

fashion as good be out of the world, as out of
the f.   FASHION, 1

fashionable For an idea…to be f. is ominous
FASHION, 3

fat Outside every f. man   OBESITY, 1
there's a thin man inside every f. man
OBESITY, 3

fate when F. summons   MORTALITY, 2

father a wise f. that knows his own child
FAMILY, 7
My f. didn't create you to arrest me
OCCUPATIONS, 92
No man is responsible for his f.   FAMILY, 8

fathers My f. can have it.   WALES, 1

fattening the things I really like…are either
immoral, illegal, or f.   PLEASURE, 3

fault one f.. It was…lousy   CRITICISM, 10

faults f., do not fear to abandon them
IMPERFECTION, 1
only confess our little f.   IMPERFECTION, 2

favour accepts a smaller as a f.
INJUSTICE, 1

fear only thing we have to f. is f. itself
COURAGE, 3

feast Paris is a moveable f.   PLACES, 7

fee doctor takes the f.   OCCUPATIONS, 49

feeding Spoon f.…teaches us nothing but the
shape of the spoon   EDUCATION, 7

feet Alan will always land on somebody's f.
HUMOUR, 7
both f. firmly planted in the air
IDEALISM, 4

feminist People call me a f. when
FEMINISM, 2

fence The…gentleman has sat so long on the
f.   NONCOMMITMENT, 2

fifty At f., everyone has the face he deserves
AGE, 15
You'll see, when you're f.   AGE, 20

fight easier to f. for one's principles
PRINCIPLES, 1
To f. and not to heed the wounds
SELFLESSNESS, 1
You cannot f. against the future
PROGRESS, 5

fighting F. is essentially a masculine idea
MEN AND WOMEN, 4

finer every baby…is a f. one   CHILDREN, 5

finger least pain in our little f.
SELFISHNESS, 1
Moving F. writes   DESTINY, 1

finished A man is…f. when he quits
DEFEAT, 2

fire what wind is to f.   LEAVING, 4

fires Husbands are like f.   WEDDINGS, 11

first Because of my title, I was the f.
COURAGE, 1

fist You cannot shake hands with a clenched f.
COMPROMISE, 1

five child of f. would understand this
SIMPLICITY, 1
practise f. things   VIRTUE, 1

flattering f. some men to endure them
TOLERANCE, 1

flattery F.…so long as you don't inhale
FLATTERY, 3

flesh the world, the f., and the devil
OCCUPATIONS, 71

flowed water f. like champagne
ABSTINENCE, 4

fly A f., Sir, may sting a stately horse
CRITICISM, 6

foe he is the sworn f. of our nation
OCCUPATIONS, 34

Folies-Bergère A psychiatrist is a man who
goes to the F.   OCCUPATIONS, 107

folk-dancing except incest and f.
EXPERIENCE, 1

follies The f. which a man regrets
REGRET, 2

follow I have to f. them, I am their leader
LEADERSHIP, 2

food F.…part of a balanced diet   FOOD, 2
On the Continent people have good f.
MANNERS, 1
wine was a farce and the f. a tragedy
FOOD, 3

fool the greatest f. may ask more
EDUCATION, 4
You can f. too many of the people
DECEPTION, 3

foolish anything very f.   PRINCIPLES, 4

fools f. decoyed into our condition
WEDDINGS, 16

football F. isn't a matter of life and death
SPORT, 9

foreign pronounce f. names as he chooses
PRONUNCIATION, 1
forget Painter...has first to f. all the roses
OCCUPATIONS, 19
Were it not better to f. REGRET, 1
forgive do not have to f. my enemies
RUTHLESSNESS, 2
f. your enemies...never forget their names
ENEMIES, 1
formidable Examinations are f.
EDUCATION, 4
fortune to make your f....let people see...it is
in their interests to promote yours
SUCCESS, 2
forty-five That should assure us of...f. minutes
of undisturbed privacy INATTENTION, 1
found Suppose it had been someone else who
f. you like this ADULTERY, 5
fox The f. knows many things
KNOWLEDGE, 1
frames The finest collection of f. ART, 5
free f. society...where it is safe to be
unpopular FREEDOM, 7
the truth shall make you f. TRUTH, 2
truth that makes men f. TRUTH, 1
We have to believe in f. will FREEDOM, 6
freedom F. is the right to tell...do not want to
hear FREEDOM, 5
f. of speech, f. of conscience, and the
prudence never to practise...them
FREEDOM, 8
f. to print...the proprietor's prejudices
MEDIA, 3
Until you've lost your reputation, you never
realize...what f. really is
REPUTATION, 2
Frenchmen to create F. in the image of
Englishmen PLACES, 3
Freud trouble with F. OCCUPATIONS, 105
friend a new f. is as new wine
FRIENDSHIP, 1
forsake not an old f. FRIENDSHIP, 1
good f. that she will throw FRIENDSHIP, 10
It takes your enemy and your f...., to hurt you
ENEMIES, 2
no man is useless while he has a f.
FRIENDSHIP, 9
save me, from the candid f. FRIENDSHIP, 2
friendly Man is the only animal...on f. terms
with the victims...he eats
HYPOCRISY, 1
friends cherish our f. not for their ability to
amuse us FRIENDSHIP, 12
Money can't buy f. MONEY, 9
none of his f. like him POPULARITY, 2
treat your f. a little better FRIENDSHIP, 5
you choose your f. FAMILY, 3
friendship f. closes its eyes FRIENDSHIP, 8
Men seem to kick f. around like a football
FRIENDSHIP, 7
frighten by God, they f. me
OCCUPATIONS, 120
frocks Her f. are built in Paris FASHION, 2
fruit Ignorance is like a delicate exotic f.
IGNORANCE, 3

fun the most f. I ever had without laughing
SEX, 2
funerals If you don't go to other men's f.
FUNERALS, 3
funny hard to be f. when you have to be clean
HUMOUR, 3
future I have seen the f. FUTURE, 4
I never think of the f. FUTURE, 3
people who live in the f. PROGRESS, 1
The f. is made of the same stuff
FUTURE, 5
You cannot fight against the f.
PROGRESS, 5

G

gaiety the only concession to g. WALES, 2
gained learning hath g. most BOOKS, 3
gainful I will undoubtedly have to seek...g.
employment LEAVING, 1
gains no g. without pains SUCCESS, 6
game It's more than a g.. It's an institution
SPORT, 4
man's idea in a card g. is war GAMES, 4
Garbo one sees in G. sober
COMPLIMENTS, 8
gatekeeper After I die, I shall return to earth
as a g. of a bordello MUSIC, 8
gather G. ye rosebuds while ye may
PRESENT, 1
generalizations All g. are dangerous
GENERALIZATIONS, 1
generation Each g. imagines itself...more
intelligent AGE, 16
genius a country full of g., but with absolutely
no talent IRELAND, 4
A g.! For thirty-seven years I've practiced...
and now they call me a g.
ACHIEVEMENT, 5
G. is one per cent inspiration
ACHIEVEMENT, 2
Nothing, except my g. BOASTS, 6
gentleman A g....wouldn't hit a woman with
his hat on CHIVALRY, 1
genuineness G. only thrives in the dark
SINCERITY, 2
geographical India is a g. term PLACES, 4
George Lloyd G. POWER, 2
giants it is by standing on the shoulders of g.
PROGRESS, 6
gift True love's the g. which God has given
/To man alone LOVE, 9
worth more than the g. GIFTS, 1
girl From birth to age eighteen, a g. needs
good parents AGE, 25
Many a man has fallen in love with a g.
LOVE, 3
see in a little g. the threat CHILDREN, 6
the hero gets the g. CENSORSHIP, 1
girls Where...boys plan for what...young g.
plan for whom
MEN AND WOMEN, 3
give To g. and not to count the cost
SELFLESSNESS, 1
given I would have g. you another
CHIVALRY, 2

giving The manner of g.   GIFTS, 1
Glasgow never played the G. Empire
    OCCUPATIONS, 105
glory paths of g. lead but to the grave
    MORTALITY, 5
gluttony G....is a sign something is eating us
    GREED, 1
go I shall be the last to g. out   COURAGE, 1
God A G. who let us prove his existence   GOD, 1
Even G. cannot change the past   PAST, 2
G. is always on the side of the big battalions
    POWER, 8
G. is on the side...of the best shots
    POWER, 9
I did not write it. G. wrote it   ACHIEVEMENT, 6
one G. only...the expense of two   GOD, 2
trust in G....and keep your powder dry
    PRUDENCE, 2
you must believe in G.   FAITH, 2
gods So many g., so many creeds
    KINDNESS, 2
godsend good servant is a real g.
    OCCUPATIONS, 110
golden perhaps, the g. rule   ABSTINENCE, 7
Goldwyn Mr G....you are only interested in art
    ART, 6
golf G....a form of moral effort   SPORT, 6
G. is a game whose aim   SPORT, 1
G. is a good walk spoiled   SPORT, 11
impossible to remember how tragic...playing
g.   SPORT, 8
good Do g. by stealth   GOOD, 4
Evil comes...like the disease; g....like the
doctor   GOOD, 2
g. eater must be a g. man   FOOD, 1
G. isn't the word   CRITICISM, 3
He who could do g....must do it in Minute
Particulars   GOOD, 1
Nothing can harm a g. man   GOOD, 6
Whenever two g. people argue over principles
    PRINCIPLES, 3
When I'm g. I'm very g.   SEX, 13
goodbyes never any good dwelling on g.
    LEAVING, 3
goodness My g. those diamonds are lovely
    GOOD, 7
gossips No one g. about...secret virtues
    GOSSIP, 1
government A g. agency is the nearest thing
to eternal life   BUREAUCRACY, 5
a g. organization could do it that quickly
    BUREAUCRACY, 2
don't make jokes...just watch the g.
    GOVERNMENT, 2
gradually Boys do not grow up g.
    CHILDREN, 3
grandfather pass my declining years
saluting...g. clocks   AGE, 14
grandmother I murdered my g. this morning
    INATTENTION, 2
grasp man's reach should exceed his g.
    AMBITION, 1
grasped journalism what will be g. at once
    OCCUPATIONS, 68

grave Between the cradle and the g.
    MORTALITY, 3
no work, nor device, nor knowledge...in the
g.   WORK, 2
paths of glory lead but to the g.
    MORTALITY, 5
great All my shows are g.   BOASTS, 3
you,...who have made me too g. for my house
    HOME, 1
No g. man lives in vain   GREATNESS, 1
To be g. is to be misunderstood
    GREATNESS, 2
green I was g. in judgment   YOUTH, 7
religious system that produced g. Chartreuse
    DRINKING, 13
grief calms one's g. by recounting it
    SORROW, 1
in much wisdom is much g.   WISDOM, 1
Should be past g.   REGRET, 3
what's past help /should be past g.
    REGRET, 3
growing G. old is like being increasingly
penalized   AGE, 17
grows Nothing g. well in the shade
    EXCUSES, 1
gun muzzle of my g. as their safest position
    HUNTING, 5
guns But it's 'Saviour of 'is country' when the
g.   OCCUPATIONS, 115

H

had you h. it in you   CHILDREN, 10
half longest h. of your life   YOUTH, 8
One h....cannot understand...the other
    PLEASURE, 1
hands don't raise your h. because I am also
nearsighted   SPEECHES, 1
To be played with both h. in the pocket
    MUSIC, 7
You cannot shake h. with a clenched fist
    COMPROMISE, 1
hanged if they were going to see me h.
    PUBLIC, 3
happens I just don't want to be there when it
h.   DEATH, 1
happiness H. is an imaginary condition
    HAPPINESS, 5
H. is like a butterfly   HAPPINESS, 2
H. is no laughing matter   HAPPINESS, 6
H.?...health and a poor memory
    HAPPINESS, 4
indispensable part of h.   HAPPINESS, 3
I thought that success spelled h.
    HAPPINESS, 2
nothing...by which so much h. is produced as
by a good tavern   DRINKING, 9
happy Ask...whether you are h.
    HAPPINESS, 1
Few people can be h. unless they hate
    HATE, 2
just as h. when I had $48 million
    MONEY, 12
Puritanism – The haunting fear that
someone...may be h.   MORALITY, 5

insect the Egyptians worshipped an i.
OCCUPATIONS, 95
inspiration Genius is one per cent i.
ACHIEVEMENT, 2
institution Marriage is a wonderful i.
MARRIAGE, 6
more than a game. It's an i.
SPORT, 4
insult A man should not i. his wife publicly
MARRIAGE, 14
insulted anyone here whom I have not i.
SPEECHES, 25
intellects highest i., like the tops of
mountains
INTELLECT, 4
intellectual i., but I found it too difficult
HUMILITY, 3
i....doesn't know how to park a bike
INTELLECT, 1
intelligence I....useless...only quality it is
INTELLECT, 3
intelligent Each generation imagines itself...
more i.
AGE, 16
stupid are cocksure...i. full of doubt
DOUBT, 1
intended i. to give you some advice
ADVICE, 2
invasion no stand can be made against i. by an
idea
IDEAS, 3
Ireland English should give I. home rule
IRELAND, 6
The problem with I.
IRELAND, 4
Irish All races have...economists, with the
exception of the I.
IRELAND, 1
I....devotion to higher arts
IRELAND, 1
The I. are a fair people
IRELAND, 3
iron the i. has entered his soul
NONCOMMITMENT, 2
irresponsible better to be i. and right
RESPONSIBILITY, 2
irritating differences in taste or opinion are i.
ARGUMENTS, 1
Italy I. a paradise for horses
ENGLAND, 1

J

jail being in a ship is being in a j.
OCCUPATIONS, 114
jealousies patience with the j....of actors
OCCUPATIONS, 5
Jefferson when Thomas J. dined alone
SPEECHES, 4
Jews The J. and Arabs should...settle their
differences
RELIGION, 1
the J. have made a contribution to the human
condition
JEWS, 2
job If two men on the same j. agree
WORK, 13
jockey the...cup is given to the j.
INJUSTICE, 2
joke j. with a double meaning
HUMOUR, 1
rich man's j.
FLATTERY, 1
jokes don't make j....just watch the
government
GOVERNMENT, 2
Forgive...my little j. on Thee
PRAYER, 2
He cannot bear old men's j.
AGE, 10
Joneses drag the J. down to my level
FAMILY, 2

journalism Christianity,...but why j.
OCCUPATIONS, 65
j.....keeps us in touch with the ignorance of
the community
OCCUPATIONS, 73
J. largely consists of saying 'Lord Jones is
dead'
OCCUPATIONS, 67
j. what will be grasped at once
OCCUPATIONS, 68
journalists j. put theirs on the front page
OCCUPATIONS, 64
joy beauty is a j. for ever
BEAUTY, 1
we could never learn to be brave...if there
were only j.
ENDURANCE, 1
judge duty of a j. is to administer justice
OCCUPATIONS, 74
j. is a law student
OCCUPATIONS, 75
j. is not supposed to know anything about the
facts of life
OCCUPATIONS, 76
judgement no one complains of his j.
JUDGMENT, 2
your j. will probably be right
JUDGMENT, 1
judges J....have their lighter moments
OCCUPATIONS, 77
just true place for a j. man is...a prison
JUSTICE, 3
justice duty of a judge is to administer j.
OCCUPATIONS, 74
J. is open to all
JUSTICE, 2
never expected j. from a company
BUSINESS, 11
The j. of my quarrel
JUSTICE, 1

K

kicked he had known many k. down stairs
LEAVING, 7
kill Nothing is ever done...until men are
prepared to k.
VIOLENCE, 2
kind being k. /Is all the sad world needs
KINDNESS, 2
I love thee for a heart that's k.
KINDNESS, 1
king He played the K. as though
CRITICISM, 2
kingdom in the k. of the well and in the k. of
the sick
ILLNESS, 3
kissed Wherever one wants to be k.
WOMEN, 5
knight end up being the shortest k. of the year
AWARDS, 3
know all /Ye k. on earth
BEAUTY, 2
What you don't k. would make a great book
IGNORANCE, 2
knowledge All k. is of itself of some value
KNOWLEDGE, 3
K. is of two kinds
KNOWLEDGE, 4
province of k. to speak
KNOWLEDGE, 2

L

labour To l. and not ask for any reward
SELFLESSNESS, 1
lack own up to a l. of humour
HUMOUR, 2
lady Being powerful is like being a l.
POWER, 3

lamb to make the lion lie down with
the l.   HUMAN NATURE, 2
lamp To keep a l. burning   CHARITY, 3
lamp-post like asking a l....about dogs
                                   OCCUPATIONS, 43
lamp-posts as a drunken man uses l.
                                   STATISTICS, 7
land they have the l. and we have the Bibles
                                   RELIGION, 6
language The English have no respect for
their l.   ENGLAND, 8
languages she speaks eighteen l.   SEX, 9
last I shall be the l. to go out   COURAGE, 1
the l. time that I will take part as an amateur
                                   FUNERALS, 1
Latin Don't quote L.   SPEECHES, 24
the Devil knows L.   CHILDREN, 8
Latins L. are tenderly enthusiastic
                                   PLACES, 6
laughed Few women care to be l. at
                                   RIDICULE, 1
most wasted of...days...is that on which one
has not l.   LAUGHTER, 1
laughing Happiness is no l. matter
                                   HAPPINESS, 6
the death of Little Nell without l.
                                   INSENSITIVITY, 1
the most fun I ever had without l.   SEX, 2
laughter I was convulsed with l.
                                   CRITICISM, 7
law judge is a l. student   OCCUPATIONS, 75
The majestic egalitarianism of the l.
                                   EQUALITY, 1
lawyer Behold a l., an honest man
                                   OCCUPATIONS, 81
course to be pursued by a l.
                                   OCCUPATIONS, 85
good l. is a bad neighbour
                                   OCCUPATIONS, 86
l. in the natural history of monsters
                                   OCCUPATIONS, 83
l. without history or literature
                                   OCCUPATIONS, 87
lawyers L. earn a living   OCCUPATIONS, 82
l....let out their brains for hire
                                   OCCUPATIONS, 79
no bad people...no good l.
                                   OCCUPATIONS, 80
unfair to believe everything...about l.
                                   OCCUPATIONS, 84
lazy have to be efficient if you're...l.
                                   LAZINESS, 1
leader I have to follow them, I am their l.
                                   LEADERSHIP, 2
learn we could never l. to be brave...if there
were only joy   ENDURANCE, 1
learning L. hath gained most   BOOKS, 3
L. is a treasure   KNOWLEDGE, 5
Their l. is like bread in a besieged town
                                   SCOTLAND, 3
least death...the l. of all evils   DEATH, 3
lechery drink...an equivocator with l.
                                   DRINKING, 14
left You just press the accelerator to the floor
and steer l.   SPORT, 12

legless critic is a l. man   OCCUPATIONS, 45
leisure few people can endure much l.
                                   LEISURE, 1
The secret of being miserable is to have l.
                                   SORROW, 2
less l. in this than meets the eye
                                   CRITICISM, 1
Specialist – A man who knows more and
more about l. and l.   EXPERTS, 2
the l. they have...the more noise they make
                                   CHARACTER, 1
letter I have made this l. longer
                                   VERBOSITY, 1
level-headed When things are steep,
remember to stay l.   SELF-CONTROL, 1
levellers Your l. wish to level *down* as far as
themselves   EQUALITY, 2
liaison l. man and partly P.R.O.   BUSINESS, 1
liar Mr. Speaker, I said the honorable member
was a l.   APOLOGIES, 2
lie A l. can be halfway round the world
                                   LYING, 1
a l. is...a very present help   LYING, 2
an honest man sent to l. abroad for...his
country   DIPLOMACY, 5
L. follows by post   APOLOGIES, 1
not to l....unless it is absolutely necessary
                                   OCCUPATIONS, 96
life death after l. does greatly please
                                   DEATH, 9
Football isn't a matter of l. and death
                                   SPORT, 9
Is l. a boon   MORTALITY, 4
L. is a maze in which we take the wrong
turning   LIFE, 3
L. is a tragedy...in close-up   LIFE, 2
L. is like a sewer   LIFE, 4
L. is what happens...while you're...making
other plans   LIFE, 5
L. would be tolerable   PLEASURE, 1
longest half of your l.   YOUTH, 8
The best part of married l. is the fights
                                   MARRIAGE, 16
The Book of L. begins   WEDDINGS, 22
the golden tree of l. is green   THEORY, 1
lightly Angels...take themselves l.
                                   SERIOUSNESS, 1
like I shall not look upon his l.
                                   COMPLIMENTS, 4
liked I'm so universally l.   POPULARITY, 1
line cancel half a L.   DESTINY, 1
lingerie Brevity is the soul of l.   CLOTHES, 3
lion to make the l. lie down with the lamb
                                   HUMAN NATURE, 2
listen privilege of wisdom to l.
                                   KNOWLEDGE, 2
listener A good l. is a good talker with a sore
throat   SPEECH, 16
literature L....something that will be read
twice   OCCUPATIONS, 68
Little Nell the death of L. without laughing
                                   INSENSITIVITY, 1
live If you l. long enough, the venerability
factor creeps in   AGE, 24
l. beyond its income   PROGRESS, 2

M. is the only adventure open to the cowardly
WEDDINGS, 21

m....not a public conveyance MARRIAGE, 7

m....resembles a pair of shears
MARRIAGE, 13

three of us in this m. ADULTERY, 3

twenty years of m. make her something like a
public building MARRIAGE, 15

married A m. couple are well suited
MARRIAGE, 10

what delight we m. people have to see
WEDDINGS, 16

marries doesn't much signify whom one m.
WEDDINGS, 17

marry as easy to m. a rich woman as a poor
woman WEDDINGS, 20

better to m. than to burn WEDDINGS, 7

no woman should m. a teetotaller
ABSTINENCE, 7

when a man should m. WEDDINGS, 4

When you're bored with yourself, m.
MARRIAGE, 9

marrying M....is like buying something...in a
shop window
MARRIAGE, 4

martyrdom M. is the test FREEDOM, 2

masculine Fighting is essentially a m. idea
MEN AND WOMEN, 4

masterpiece Who am I to tamper with a m.
BOASTS, 7

masters Buy old m. ART, 3

matinée Robert Houdin who...invented the...
theater m. SPEECHES, 26

maturity m. is only a short break in
adolescence AGE, 9

maunder m. and mumble PUBLIC, 2

May darling buds of M. COMPLIMENTS, 5

maze Life is a m. LIFE, 3

measles Love's like the m. LOVE, 6

medicines Doctors...prescribe m. of which
they know little OCCUPATIONS, 57

mediocre Women want m. men
MEN AND WOMEN, 7

medium A m....neither rare nor well done
MEDIA, 1

meek The m. do not inherit the earth
HUMILITY, 2

meet Two may talk...yet never really m.
FRIENDSHIP, 3

memorandum A m. is written
BUREAUCRACY, 1

memory Everyone complains of his m.
JUDGMENT, 2

good storyteller is a person who has a good
m. SPEECHES, 14

Happiness?...health and a poor m.
HAPPINESS, 4

men Great m. are almost always bad m.
POWER, 1

It's not the m. in my life that count
SEX, 12

M. don't understand anything about women
MEN AND WOMEN, 2

M. will confess HUMOUR, 2

schemes o' mice an' m. FAILURE, 1

The m. that women marry...a mystery
MARRIAGE, 5

Why are women...so much more interesting
to m. MEN AND WOMEN, 11

merger trying to pull off a m. between Heaven
and Hell BUSINESS, 13

messages important m. from the brain
SPEECHES, 12

mice schemes o' m. an' men FAILURE, 1

middle people who stay in the m. of the road
NONCOMMITMENT, 1

mike I'm being amplified by the m.
SPEECHES, 2

militant I am an optimist, unrepentant and m.
OPTIMISM, 3

military When the m. man approaches
OCCUPATIONS, 117

million man who has a m. dollars
MONEY, 2

Milton after Shakespeare and M. are forgotten
CRITICISM, 9

Malt does more than M. can DRINKING, 7

mind m., once expanded...never returns to its
original size IDEAS, 2

m. treats a new idea...same way the body
IDEAS, 5

prodigious quantity of m. INDECISION, 1

minute He who would do good...must do it in
M. Particulars GOOD, 1

minutes sixty m. an hour TIME, 1

mirror The secret of being m. is to have
woman looks in her m. MEN AND WOMEN, 10

miserable The secret of being m. is to have
leisure SORROW, 2

misery greatest m. is a battle gained
VICTORY, 2

misfortunes strong enough to bear the m. of
others MISFORTUNE, 2

mistakes The man who makes no m.
MISTAKES, 4

mistresses a better price than old m.
ART, 1

Wives are young men's m. WEDDINGS, 3

modest man who has no talent and is m.
TALENT, 1

never known a truly m. person to be...shy
SHYNESS, 2

money Brigands demand your m. or your life
WOMEN, 4

except for large sums of m. RIDICULE, 1

If you can...count your m. you are not...rich
man MONEY, 5

innocently employed than in getting m.
MONEY, 6

M. can't buy friends MONEY, 9

M. doesn't make you happy MONEY, 12

M. is like manure MONEY, 10

M. is like muck MONEY, 3

M., it turned out, was exactly like sex
MONEY, 4

the poor person...thinks m. would help
MONEY, 7

When an actor has m. OCCUPATIONS, 3

You can be young without m.
MONEY, 17

monogamy M. is the same thing
MARRIAGE, 1
monsters lawyer in the natural history of m.
OCCUPATIONS, 74
moon For years politicians have promised the m.
ACHIEVEMENT, 4
moral Love is m. even without…marriage
WEDDINGS, 14
M. indignation is in most cases 2 percent m.
MORALITY, 9
m. is what you feel good after
MORALITY, 4
morality M. consists in suspecting
MORALITY, 7
M. is…expediency in a long white dress
MORALITY, 1
new m.…the old immorality condoned
MORALITY, 8
No m. can be founded on authority
MORALITY, 2
more Specialist – A man who knows m. and m. about less and less
EXPERTS, 2
morn From m. to night, my friend
ENDURANCE, 4
morning 'Tis always m. somewhere
BEGINNING, 3
mortal doctor found…last disorder m.
OCCUPATIONS, 50
mould If you cannot m. yourself
TOLERANCE, 2
mountains highest intellects, like the tops of m.
INTELLECT, 4
mouse leave room for the m.
EXCESS, 1
mouth butter wouldn't melt in her m.
INSULTS, 1
impossible for an Englishman to open his m.
PLACES, 17
moving The M. Finger writes
DESTINY, 1
muck Money is like m.
MONEY, 3
mumble maunder and m.
PUBLIC, 2
murder men will confess to treason, m., arson, false teeth
HUMOUR, 2
murdered I m. my grandmother this morning
INATTENTION, 2
m. his parents then pleaded for mercy
HYPOCRISY, 3
music keep swinging after the m. had finished
NAKEDNESS, 1
The English may not like m.
MUSIC, 3
The m. teacher came twice each week
MUSIC, 1
Van Gogh's ear for m.
INSULTS, 6
mystery a riddle wrapped in a m. inside an enigma
PLACES, 5
The men that women marry…a m.
MARRIAGE, 5

N

name-dropper One must not be a n.
SNOBBERY, 2
nation he is the sworn foe of our n.
OCCUPATIONS, 34
No n. was ever ruined by trade
BUSINESS, 4
nature drive away N. with a pitchfork
NATURE, 1

N. is usually wrong
NATURE, 3
N. might stand up and say…'This was a man!'
NOBILITY, 1
natural If sex is such a n. phenomenon
SEX, 8
nearsighted don't raise your hands because I am also n.
SPEECHES, 1
neck equipping us with a n.
COURAGE, 2
Nell the death of Little N. without laughing
INSENSITIVITY, 1
nervous approaching n. breakdown
WORK, 10
new There are no n. truths
TRUTH, 6
You suddenly understand something…in a n. way
EDUCATION, 8
Youth is something very n.
YOUTH, 1
newspaper good n.,…is a nation talking to itself
OCCUPATIONS, 70
Once a n. touches a story
OCCUPATIONS, 69
With the n. strike on
OBITUARIES, 1
newspapers It's the n. I can't stand
MEDIA, 2
nice amazing how n. people
LEAVING, 2
Be n. to people on your way up
WORK, 8
night From morn to n., my friend
ENDURANCE, 4
Nixon N.…would cut down a redwood tree
OCCUPATIONS, 99
no she can't say 'N.' in any of them
SEX, 9
noble the n. living and the n. dead
NOBILITY, 2
noise A loud n. at one end
CHILDREN, 7
the less they have…the more n. they make
CHARACTER, 1
they…love the n. it makes
MUSIC, 3
noisy The people would be just as n.
PUBLIC, 3
nonconformist a n. like everybody else
CONFORMITY, 2
a man must be a n.
CONFORMITY, 1
nose A custom loathsome to the eye, hateful to the n.
SMOKING, 3
nothing Certainly, there is n. else here to enjoy
PARTIES, 3
doing n. for each other
FRIENDSHIP, 4
from n. to a state of extreme poverty
POVERTY, 3
have n. whatever to do with it
DEATH, 8
N., except my genius
BOASTS, 6
When you have n. to say, say n.
SPEECH, 3
novel When I want to read a n.
OCCUPATIONS, 25
nuisance exchange of one n. for another n.
PROGRESS, 3
nurses old men's n.
WEDDINGS, 3

O

oaths O. are but words
SPEECH, 2
obey born to o.
LEADERSHIP, 1
occupation only man…apologizing for his o.
BUSINESS, 8
odious One is not superior…because one sees the world in an o. light
CYNICISM, 1

office not describe holding public o.
                                        LEAVING, 1
  o. sanctifies the holder   POWER, 1
offspring Heaven has granted me no o.
                                        BOASTS, 5
old Growing o. is like being increasingly
        penalized   AGE, 17
  He cannot bear o. men's jokes   AGE, 10
  I prefer o. age to the alternative   AGE, 5
  man…as o. as the woman he feels
                                        AGE, 12
  O. men are dangerous   AGE, 23
  the o. have reminiscences   AGE, 19
  the o. have rubbed it into the young that they
        are wiser   AGE, 13
  young can do for the o. is to shock them
                                        AGE, 21
older I was so much o. then   YOUTH, 3
  make way for an o. man   LEAVING, 9
  to go on getting o.   SURVIVAL, 1
one The number o. book…was written by a
        committee   BUREAUCRACY, 4
one-handed Give me a o. economist
                                        ECONOMICS, 4
open I declare this thing o. – whatever it is
                                        SPEECHES, 6
  mind is…so o. that nothing is retained
                                        STUPIDITY, 1
opera o. isn't what it used to be   MUSIC, 5
opinion One often contradicts an o.
                                        ARGUMENTS, 3
  the English think of an o. as something…to
        hide   ENGLAND, 3
opportunities One can present people with o.
                                        OPPORTUNITY, 2
opportunity Equality of o.   OPPORTUNITY, 3
  follies…he didn't commit when he had the o.
                                        REGRET, 2
optimist an o.…fills up his crossword puzzle
        in ink   OPTIMISM, 2
  an o. who carries a raincoat   PRUDENCE, 3
  I am an o., unrepentant and militant
                                        OPTIMISM, 3
  The o. proclaims   OPTIMISM, 1
oral a terrific story about o. contraception
                                        CONTRACEPTION, 2
orators What o. lack in depth   SPEECHES, 19
ordering the better o. of the universe
                                        UNIVERSE, 2
ordinary One machine can do the work of fifty
        o. men   TECHNOLOGY, 2
organ my second favourite o.   SEX, 1
organization a government o. could do it that
        quickly   BUREAUCRACY, 2
orgies Home is heaven and o. are vile
                                        DEBAUCHERY, 2
others The sort…who lives for o.   DUTY, 2
original An o. writer is not   ORIGINALITY, 2
overexposure she should catch a cold on o.
                                        TRUTH, 3
oyster bold man that first eat an o.
                                        COURAGE, 4

P

pain least p. in our little finger
                                        SELFISHNESS, 1
  The p. passes, but the beauty remains
                                        ENDURANCE, 3
painted Most women are not so young as they
        are p.   WOMEN, 3
painter difficult for a truly creative p. to paint a
        rose   OCCUPATIONS, 19
  never been a boy p.   OCCUPATIONS, 16
painters p. who transform the sun into a
        yellow spot   OCCUPATIONS, 21
pallbearer get my exercise acting as a p.
                                        LAZINESS, 2
pants There were times my p. were so thin
                                        POVERTY, 6
  Your eyes shine like the p.
                                        COMPLIMENTS, 2
paper Where were you fellows when the p.
        was blank   OCCUPATIONS, 58
paradise England is a p. for women
                                        PLACES, 3
paranoid Even a p. can have enemies
                                        ENEMIES, 2
parents by defying their p. and copying one
        another   YOUTH, 2
  Don't hold your p. up to contempt
                                        FAMILY, 9
  From birth to age eighteen, a girl needs good
        p.   AGE, 25
  P.…a disappointment to their children
                                        FAMILY, 6
  P. learn a lot   CHILDREN, 13
  precautions to avoid having p.   FAMILY, 1
  the way p. obey their children   FAMILY, 10
Parliament P. is the longest running farce
                                        GOVERNMENT, 3
parting P. is such sweet sorrow
                                        LEAVING, 12
party best number for a dinner p. is two
                                        PARTIES, 2
pass I shall not p. this way again
                                        MORTALITY, 6
  young have aspirations that never come to p.
                                        AGE, 19
past Even God cannot change the p.   PAST, 2
  events in the p.…probably never happened
                                        HISTORY, 3
  Keep off your thoughts from things that are p.
                                        PAST, 6
  looking forward to the p.   NOSTALGIA, 1
  people who live in the p.   PROGRESS, 1
  The only thing I regret about my p. life
                                        AGE, 2
  The p., at least, is secure   PAST, 7
  The p. is a foreign country   PAST, 3
  The p. is the only dead thing   PAST, 5
  what's p. help Should be p. grief
                                        REGRET, 3
patience strange…that the years teach us p.
                                        PATIENCE, 3
patient good p. is one who
                                        OCCUPATIONS, 52
  the Fury of a p. man   PATIENCE, 1

patients Doctors think a lot of p. are cured
OCCUPATIONS, 51

patriot He was a great p....provided...that he really is dead
COMPLIMENTS, 9

patriotism P. is the last refuge
PATRIOTISM, 2

pay better...not vow, than...vow and not p.
PROMISES, 1

peace P....a period of cheating
PEACE, 1
prepare...for p. like retarded pygmies
PEACE, 4

peerage When I want a p., I shall buy one
AWARDS, 2

pen less brilliant p. than mine
BOASTS, 1

people Be nice to p. on your way up
WORK, 8
It is with...p. as with...bottles
CHARACTER, 1
p. attached to cats
ANIMALS, 5
p. who stay in the middle of the road
NONCOMMITMENT, 1
The Lord prefers common-looking p.
APPEARANCE, 5
The p. would be just as noisy
PUBLIC, 3
You can fool too many of the p.
DECEPTION, 3

perfection P. has one grave defect
PERFECTION, 1

performance it takes away the p.
DRINKING, 14

perils smile at p. past
PAST, 4

perish better to p. than to continue schoolmastering
OCCUPATIONS, 125

persecution Nothing can render them popular but p.
OCCUPATIONS, 37

perversion that melancholy sexual p. known as continence
ABSTINENCE, 6

pervert Once: a philosopher; twice: a p.
DEBAUCHERY, 3

pessimist A p....looks both ways before crossing
PESSIMISM, 4
the p. fears this is true
OPTIMISM, 1

pessimists p....end up desiring the things they fear
PESSIMISM, 3

petticoat turned out of the Realm in my p.
SELF-RELIANCE, 1

philosopher never yet p. /That could endure the toothache
ENDURANCE, 5
Once: a p.; twice: a pervert
DEBAUCHERY, 3

philosophy for a...p. to be substantially true
PHILOSOPHY, 2
The point of p. is
PHILOSOPHY, 1

physicians too many p.
MEDICINE, 1

Piccadilly Crossing P. Circus
LONDON, 3

pickle weaned on a p.
APPEARANCE, 6

pimp editor should have a p. for a brother
OCCUPATIONS, 59

piss I can p. the old boy
BOASTS, 4

pitchfork drive Nature away with a p.
NATURE, 1

place Home is the p. where
HOME, 2

planet it fell on the wrong p.
WEAPONS, 1

plans Life is what happens...while you're making other p.
LIFE, 5

what a man still p....shows the...injustice in his death
DEATH, 4

plays p. about rape, sodomy and drug addiction
THEATRE, 1

playwright drama critic is a person who surprises the p.
OCCUPATIONS, 44
p. to be urged to do something
FLATTERY, 2

please I...do what I p.
FREEDOM, 1
They...say what they p.
FREEDOM, 1

pleasure gave p. to the spectators
MORALITY, 5
p. of fishing them out again
FRIENDSHIP, 10

pleasures being ill...one of the greatest p. of life
ILLNESS, 1
One half...cannot understand the p.
PLEASURE, 1
The English take their p. sadly
ENGLAND, 9

pocket To be played with both hands in the p.
MUSIC, 7

poem I do not think this p. will reach its destination
CRITICISM, 11

poetry read a little p. sometimes
IGNORANCE, 1

police I'm not against the p.
OCCUPATIONS, 90

policemen P. are numbered
OCCUPATIONS, 91

politeness Punctuality is the p. of kings
PROMPTNESS, 1

politician at home you're just a p.
OCCUPATIONS, 97

politicians p. will always be there
OCCUPATIONS, 93

politics first rule of p. is
OCCUPATIONS, 96
P. come from man.
OCCUPATIONS, 103
P. is the art of preventing people from taking part
OCCUPATIONS, 89
p. was the second lowest profession
OCCUPATIONS, 98

poor being p....takes up all your time
POVERTY, 1
only the p....forbidden to beg
POVERTY, 2
p. have no right to the property of the rich
POVERTY, 4
the p. person...thinks money would help
MONEY, 7

portrait person grow to look like his p.
OCCUPATIONS, 17

posterity doing something for p.
PAST, 1

postures It requires one to assume such indecent p.
SPORT, 13

poultry A p. matter
MONEY, 8

poverty from nothing to a state of extreme p.
POVERTY, 3
p. is the mother of crime
CRIME, 2

powder trust in God...and keep your p. dry
PRUDENCE, 2

power Men of p. have not time to read
POWER, 5
People have p. when
POWER, 6
P. tends to corrupt
POWER, 1
wrong sort of people are always in p.
POWER, 10

You only have p. over people   POWER, 7
powerful   Being p. is like being a lady
   POWER, 3
powers   Headmasters have p.
   OCCUPATIONS, 126
practiced   For thirty-seven years I've p....and
now they call me a genius   ACHIEVEMENT, 5
praise   To refuse p.   PRAISE, 3
Watch how a man takes p.   PRAISE, 1
praising   advantage of...p....oneself
   PRAISE, 2
pray   p. for you at St Paul's   PRAYER, 3
prejudice   I am free of all p.   HATE, 1
prejudices   Common sense is the collection of
p.   PREJUDICE, 2
freedom to print...the proprietor's p.
   MEDIA, 3
Show me a critic without p.   CRITICISM, 8
President   American...prepared to run for P.
   OCCUPATIONS, 102
one thing about being P.   POWER, 4
pretty   There's only one p. child
   CHILDREN, 12
preventing   Politics is the art of p. people from
taking part   OCCUPATIONS, 101
price   a better p. than old mistresses
   ART, 3
the p. of everything and the value of nothing
   CYNICISM, 2
princes   mine were p. of the earth   JEWS, 1
principle   agree to a thing in p.
   AGREEMENT, 1
except from some strong p.   PRINCIPLES, 4
the p. seems the same   PLACES, 2
principles   compelled to rise above his p.
   PRINCIPLE, 2
easier to fight for one's p.   PRINCIPLES, 1
Whenever two good people argue over p.
   PRINCIPLES, 3
print   big p. giveth   BUSINESS, 9
printers   those books by which the p. have lost
   BOOKS, 3
prison   Anyone who has been to...public
school will...feel...at home in p.
   EDUCATION, 13
place for a just man is...a p.   JUSTICE, 3
prisoners   If this is the way Queen Victoria
treats her p.   COMPLAINTS, 2
p. of addiction and p. of envy
   MATERIALISM, 1
privacy   That should assure us of...forty-five
minutes of undisturbed p.   INATTENTION, 1
P.R.O.   liaison man and partly P.
   BUSINESS, 1
professor   p. of poetry is rather like being a
Kentucky colonel
   OCCUPATIONS, 123
profit   Drop...what tomorrow may bring...
count as p. every day that Fate allows you
   PRESENT, 2
progress   All p. is based   PROGRESS, 2
What we call p. is   PROGRESS, 3
prohibition   Communism is like p.
   COMMUNISM, 2

promise   A p. made is a debt unpaid
   PROMISES, 2
rarely...one can see in a little boy the p. of a
man   CHILDREN, 6
promising   they first call p.   TALENT, 2
pronounce   p. foreign names as he chooses
   PRONUNCIATION, 1
property   poor have no right to the p. of the
rich   POVERTY, 4
thieves respect p.   CRIME, 1
prophecies   bring about the verification of his
own p.   PROPHECY, 1
prosper   Treason doth never p.
   BETRAYAL, 2
protect   p. the writer   BUREAUCRACY, 1
proud   no guarantee...you will not be p. of the
feat   HUMILITY, 1
prudence   freedom of speech, freedom of
conscience, and the p. never to practise...
them   FREEDOM, 8
psychiatrist   A p. is a man who goes to the
Folies-Bergère   OCCUPATIONS, 107
P.: A man who asks you a lot of expensive
questions   OCCUPATIONS, 104
see a p. out of boredom   OCCUPATIONS, 106
public   a more mean, stupid...ungrateful
animal than the p.   PUBLIC, 4
give the p. what they want to see and they'll
come out for it   FUNERALS, 6
not describe holding p. office   LEAVING, 1
The P. is an old woman   PUBLIC, 1
twenty years of marriage make her...like a p.
building   MARRIAGE, 15
public school   Anyone who has been to...p.
will...feel...at home in prison
   EDUCATION, 13
pulse   worse occupations...than feeling a
woman's p.   OCCUPATIONS, 55
punctuality   P. is the politeness of kings
   PROMPTNESS, 1
P....virtue of the bored   PROMPTNESS, 2
punished   Am I not p. enough in not being
born an Englishman   ENGLAND, 10
punishing   p. anyone who comes between
them   MARRIAGE, 13
pupils   teacher defends his p. against
   OCCUPATIONS, 122
pure   p. as the driven slush   PURITY, 1
Puritan   The P. hated bear-baiting
   MORALITY, 5
Puritanism   P. – The haunting fear that
someone...may be happy   MORALITY, 6
pygmies   prepare...for peace like retarded p.
   PEACE, 4

Q

quantity   a prodigious q. of mind
   INDECISION, 1
quarrel   q. at the same time   MARRIAGE, 10
The justice of my q.   JUSTICE, 1
quarrelled   I did not know that we had ever q.
   ARGUMENTS, 1
queue   An Englishman...forms an orderly q. of
one   ENGLAND, 5
quit   try, try again. Then q.   REALISM, 1

quits A man is…finished when he q.

DEFEAT, 2

quotations get one's q. very slightly wrong

QUOTATIONS, 1

R

racket it ruins the whole r. FEMINISM, 1

radical A r. is a man IDEALISM, 4

radio I had the r. on NAKEDNESS, 2

raincoat an optimist who carries a r.

PRUDENCE, 3

Randolph the only part of R. that was not malignant INSULTS, 5

reach a man's r. should exceed his grasp

AMBITION, 1

read expect a man to retain everything…he has ever r. MEMORY, 2

I've just r. that I am dead OBITUARIES, 2

Men of power have not time to r.

POWER, 5

When I want to r. a novel OCCUPATIONS, 25

reader not to inform the r. BUREAUCRACY, 1

reading I shall lose no time in r. it

EXCUSES, 2

realm turned out of the R. in my petticoat

SELF-RELIANCE, 1

reasoners most plausible r. THINKING, 1

reasons never give your r. JUDGMENT, 1

There are five r. we should drink

DRINKING, 1

rebel how to r. and conform at the same time

YOUTH, 2

recession R. when…neighbour loses his job

ECONOMICS, 2

recounting calms one's grief by r. it

SORROW, 1

redwood Nixon…would cut down a r. tree

OCCUPATIONS, 99

refuge Idleness…the r. of weak minds

IDLENESS, 1

Patriotism is the last r. PATRIOTISM, 2

refuse To r. praise PRAISE, 3

register I want to r. a complaint

COMPLAINTS, 1

regret remember and r. REGRET, 1

regrets The follies which a man r.

REGRET, 2

relations Fate chooses your r. FAMILY, 3

remember r. and regret REGRET, 1

we shall be glad to r. even these hardships

ENDURANCE, 6

reminiscences the old have r. AGE, 19

remorse r. for what you have thought about your wife MARRIAGE, 11

render husband r. unto the wife due benevolence WEDDINGS, 6

repartee Violence is the r. of the illiterate

VIOLENCE, 1

repetition constant r. will finally succeed in imprinting an idea PUBLIC, 5

reporter A r. is a man who has renounced everything OCCUPATIONS, 71

reputation ever written out of r. but by himself

REPUTATION, 1

Until you've lost your r., you never realize… what freedom really is

REPUTATION, 2

respect now I don't have to r. anybody

AGE, 4

The English have no r. for their language

ENGLAND, 8

responsibility In dreams begins r.

RESPONSIBILITY, 1

no sense of r. at the other CHILDREN, 7

responsible No man is r. for his father

FAMILY, 8

r. and wrong RESPONSIBILITY, 2

rest get rid of the r. of her WOMEN, 12

To toil and not to seek for r.

SELFLESSNESS, 1

retirement cold wind blows…That's r.

LEAVING, 8

R. from the concert world LEAVING, 6

retires When a man r. LEAVING, 13

retrograde All that is human must r.

PROGRESS, 4

Revelations It ends with R. WEDDINGS, 22

revenue name a virtue that brings in as much r. SMOKING, 5

reward The r. of a thing well done

SUCCESS, 4

To labour and not ask for any r.

SELFLESSNESS, 1

Vice is its own r. VICE, 1

rheumatism don't believe in r. and true love

SCEPTICISM, 1

rhythm couples who use the r. method

CONTRACEPTION, 1

rich A r. man…isn't afraid to ask

MONEY, 1

A r. man's joke FLATTERY, 1

as easy to marry a r. woman as a poor woman

WEDDINGS, 20

as well off as if he were r. MONEY, 2

If you can…count your money you are not…r. man MONEY, 5

poor have no right to the property of the r.

POVERTY, 4

the wretchedness of being r. MONEY, 14

you have to live with r. people MONEY, 14

riddle a r. wrapped in a mystery inside an enigma PLACES, 5

right Always do r. RIGHT, 2

better to be irresponsible and r.

RESPONSIBILITY, 1

Every man has a r. to utter what he thinks truth FREEDOM, 2

gain great eminence without ever being r.

ECONOMICS, 1

I disapprove of what you say, but I will defend…your r. to say it FREEDOM, 9

not clever but…always r.

SELF-CONFIDENCE, 1

our country, r. or wrong PATRIOTISM, 1

ring Don't carry away that arm till I have…my r. PRACTICALITY, 1

Ritz like the R. hotel JUSTICE, 2

river One does not insult the r. god

PRUDENCE, 1

road Does the r. wind up-hill
ENDURANCE, 4
roads Two r. diverged in a wood
CHOICE, 1
robbed when you've r. a man of everything
POWER, 7
romance Twenty years of r. makes a woman
look like a ruin MARRIAGE, 15
room There is always r. at the top
AMBITION, 5
who sneaked into my r. at three o'clock this
morning COMPLAINTS, 1
rose difficult for a truly creative painter to
paint a r. OCCUPATIONS, 19
rosebuds Gather ye r. while ye may
PRESENT, 1
roses days of wine and r. MORTALITY, 1
I would like my r. to see you
COMPLIMENTS, 6
ruin Twenty years of romance makes a woman
look like a r. MARRIAGE, 15
rule A little r., a little sway MORTALITY, 3
English should give Ireland home r.
IRELAND, 6

S

sad being kind /Is all the s. world needs
KINDNESS, 2
safety s. is in our speed HASTE, 1
said they do not know what they have s.
SPEECHES, 13
sailor wonder…sane man can be a s.
OCCUPATIONS, 113
sailors s. get money like horses
OCCUPATIONS, 118
salad My s. days YOUTH, 7
salary s. of the chief executive…not a market
award for achievement BUSINESS, 5
this is the week I earn my s. MERIT, 1
same principle seems the s. PLACES, 2
Samuel When they circumcised Herbert S.
INSULTS, 3
sardines Life is…like a tin of s. LIFE, 1
sat The…gentleman has s. so long on the
fence NONCOMMITMENT, 2
Saviour But it's 'S. of 'is country' when the
guns OCCUPATIONS, 115
say cannot s. what you have to s. in twenty
minutes SPEECHES, 10
say what you have to s., and then sit down
SPEECHES, 24
They are to s. what they please
FREEDOM, 1
they do not know what they are going to s.
SPEECHES, 13
When you have nothing to s. SPEECH, 3
saying when…speaking, they do not know
what they are s. SPEECHES, 13
scarce S., sir. Mighty s. WOMEN, 11
scene artist who always paints the same s.
pleases the public OCCUPATIONS, 23
sceptic too much of a s. to deny…anything
SCEPTICISM, 2
schemes best laid s. o' mice an' men
FAILURE, 1

school never gone to s. may steal from a
freight car EDUCATION, 9
nothing on earth…so horrible as a s.
EDUCATION, 10
schooling s. interfere with my education
EDUCATION, 11
schoolmaster average s. is…essentially an ass
OCCUPATIONS, 130
s. should have an atmosphere of awe
OCCUPATIONS, 124
schoolmastering better to perish than to
continue s. OCCUPATIONS, 125
schoolmasters most s. are idiots
OCCUPATIONS, 132
science drawback that s.…invented after I left
school SCIENCE, 1
s. is said to be useful if SCIENCE, 4
Scotchman Much may be made of a S.
SCOTLAND, 2
Scotsman S. on the make SCOTLAND, 1
to distinguish between a S. with a grievance
SCOTLAND, 4
seas port after stormy s. DEATH, 9
season a perfectly ghastly s.…for you Spanish
dancers CHARITY, 1
seat offering my s. to three ladies
OBESITY, 2
seated Be sincere, be brief, be s.
SPEECHES, 20
sea-water Wealth is like s. GREED, 2
secret a s. in the Oxford sense SECRECY, 2
a s.…whispered everywhere SECRECY, 1
secure The past, at least, is s. PAST, 7
see To s. ourselves as others s. us
APPEARANCE, 4
You'll s. when you're fifty AGE, 20
seek I will undoubtedly have to s.…gainful
employment LEAVING, 1
To toil and not to s. for rest
SELFLESSNESS, 1
sees What, when drunk, one s. in other
women COMPLIMENTS, 8
self-made A s. man…believes in luck
SELF-MADE MEN, 3
a s. man who owed his lack of success to
nobody SELF-MADE MEN, 2
sense Common s. is the collection of
prejudices PREJUDICE, 2
wonderful to see persons of the best s.…
shuffling and dividing a pack of cards
GAMES, 1
sentiment s. that rubs you up the wrong way
SENTIMENTALITY, 2
servant good s. is a real godsend
OCCUPATIONS, 110
servants employers wanting all sorts of s.
OCCUPATIONS, 108
serve also s. who only stand and wait
SERVICE, 1
service I will see you in the vestry after s.
OCCUPATIONS, 37
small s. is true s. SERVICE, 2
seventy Oh to be s. again AGE, 6
sex Continental people have s. life
ENGLAND, 6

sparrow It is a city where you can see a s. fall
                                              IRELAND, 5
speak Begin low, s. slow   SPEECHES, 7
  I only s. right on   SPEECHES, 22
  province of knowledge to s.   KNOWLEDGE, 2
  time to think before I s.   SPEECH, 4
speaking Adepts in the s. trade
                                        SPEECHES, 11
  when…s., they do not know what they are
  saying   SPEECHES, 12
specialist S. – A man who knows more and
  more about less and less   EXPERTS, 2
speech A s. is like a love affair
                                        SPEECHES, 18
  freedom of s., freedom of conscience, and the
  prudence never to practise…them
                                        FREEDOM, 8
  I dreamt that I was making a s.
                                        SPEECHES, 15
  indignation makes an excellent s.
                                        SPEECHES, 16
  let thy s. be short   SPEECHES, 9
  The most precious things in s.   SPEECH, 13
  The true use of s.   SPEECH, 6
  three weeks to prepare a good impromptu s.
                                        SPEECHES, 23
speechmaker fellow who says, 'I'm no s.'
                                        SPEECHES, 17
speed safety is in our s.   HASTE, 1
spoon S. feeding…teaches us nothing but the
  shape of the s.   EDUCATION, 7
sport man wants to murder a tiger he calls it s.
                                        HUNTING, 4
  the s. of kings   HUNTING, 6
sportsman destroys one of the works of God
  we call him a s.   HUNTING, 3
spurts They move forward in s.
                                        CHILDREN, 3
stairs he had known many kicked down s.
                                        LEAVING, 7
star Being a s. has made it possible
                                        FAME, 2
stars beauty of a thousand s.   BEAUTY, 3
statesman abroad you're a s.
                                        OCCUPATIONS, 97
statistics S. will prove anything
                                        STATISTICS, 2
  uses s. as a drunken man   STATISTICS, 1
statue there's a s. inside every block of stone
                                        OBESITY, 3
steal man who has never gone to school may
  s.   CRIME, 3
  man who will s. for me will s. from me
                                        LOYALTY, 1
stealth Do good by s.   GOOD, 4
steel more than complete s.   JUSTICE, 1
steep When things are s., remember to stay
  level-headed   SELF-CONTROL, 1
steer You just press the accelerator to the
  floor and s. left   SPORT, 12
step first s.…is difficult
                                        BEGINNING, 1
stick meant us to s. it out   COURAGE, 2
sticks Casting a ball at three straight s.
                                        SPORT, 5

stomach deep sounds from the s.
                                        SPEECHES, 12
  use a little wine for thy s.'s sake
                                        DRINKING, 4
  You can't think rationally on an empty s.
                                        THINKING, 2
stop S. all the clocks   FUNERALS, 2
stops The buck s. here   RESPONSIBILITY, 3
story interesting thing about any s.
                                        OCCUPATIONS, 72
storyteller good s. is a person who has a good
  memory   SPEECHES, 14
strange pass my declining years saluting s.
  women   AGE, 13
strangled down which ideas are lured and…s.
                                        BUREAUCRACY, 3
streets S. full of water   PLACES, 1
strong s. enough to bear the misfortunes of
  others   MISFORTUNE, 2
study much s. is a weariness of the flesh
                                        BOOKS, 1
stuff The future is made of the same s.
                                        FUTURE, 5
stupid At sixteen I was s., confused
                                        AGE, 9
  s. are cocksure…intelligent full of doubt
                                        DOUBT, 1
Stygian resembling the horrible S. smoke of
  the pit   SMOKING, 3
subject Her Majesty is not a s.
                                        ROYALTY, 1
  poetry…not really a s. one can profess
                                        OCCUPATIONS, 123
succeed It is not enough to s.
                                        RUTHLESSNESS, 3
success a self-made man who owed his lack
  of s. to nobody   SELF-MADE MEN, 2
  I thought that s. spelled happiness
                                        HAPPINESS, 2
  no very lively hope of s.   PRAYER, 3
  only place where s. comes before work
                                        SUCCESS, 5
  The penalty of s.   SUCCESS, 1
  two to make a marriage a s.   MARRIAGE, 12
successful It was very s.   WEAPONS, 1
suit in a light so dim he would not have
  chosen s. by it   LOVE, 3
suitable no s. material to work on
                                        LEADERSHIP, 1
summons when Fate s.   MORTALITY, 2
sun Fear no more the heat o' the s.
                                        LEAVING, 11
sunbeams If s. were weapons   WAR, 3
superior One is not s.…because one sees the
  world in an odious light   CYNICISM, 1
superstitions s. of the human mind
                                        PURITY, 4
support s. me when…wrong   SUPPORT, 1
  s. rather than illumination   STATISTICS, 1
swan What time is the next s.   MISTAKES, 6
sway A little rule, a little s.   MORTALITY, 3
swinging keep s. after the music had finished
                                        NAKEDNESS, 1

T

tailor I go to a better t. than any of you
CLOTHES, 1

'taint 't. yours, and 't. mine
MONEY, 15

take They have to t. you in
HOME, 2

talent a country full of genius, but with absolutely no t.
IRELAND, 4

man who has no t. and is modest
TALENT, 1

the most extraordinary collection of t.
SPEECHES, 4

There is no such thing as a great t. without great will-power
ACHIEVEMENT, 1

talk Two may t....yet never really meet
FRIENDSHIP, 3

talker A good listener is a good t. with a sore throat
SPEECH, 16

talkers fluent t.
THINKING, 1

talking good newspaper,...is a nation t. to itself
OCCUPATIONS, 70

I wouldn't be...t. to someone like you
SNOBBERY, 1

T. and eloquence are not the same
SPEECH, 10

tamper Who am I to t. with a masterpiece
BOASTS, 7

tapeworm newspaper editor and...a fellow with a t.
OCCUPATIONS, 60

Tasmanians the T....are now extinct
ADULTERY, 4

tavern A t. chair is the throne
DRINKING, 8

nothing...by which so much happiness is produced as by a good t.
DRINKING, 9

taxes Death and t. and childbirth
CHILDREN, 9

taxi done almost every human activity inside a t.
BOASTS, 2

teacher art of the t. to awaken joy
OCCUPATIONS, 127

t. affects eternity
OCCUPATIONS, 121

t. defends his pupils against
OCCUPATIONS, 122

t. is one who
OCCUPATIONS, 131

t. should have maximal authority
OCCUPATIONS, 133

teachers give the t. stipends worthy of the pains
OCCUPATIONS, 129

looks back with appreciation to the brilliant t.
OCCUPATIONS, 128

teetotaller no woman should marry a t.
ABSTINENCE, 7

teetotallers T. lack the sympathy
ABSTINENCE, 3

tell do not t. them so
WISDOM, 2

t. it to...one person at a time
SECRECY, 2

tells man never t. you anything
ARGUMENTS, 4

temptation I never resist t.
TEMPTATION, 1

The only way to get rid of a t.
TEMPTATION, 2

ten our dykes,...are t. feet deep
BOASTS, 8

test Martyrdom is the t.
FREEDOM, 2

thank Don't bother to t. me
CHARITY, 1

theologians One cathedral is worth a hundred t.
RELIGION, 2

theory t. is all grey
THEORY, 1

thin there's a t. man inside every fat man
OBESITY, 3

There were times my pants were so t.
POVERTY, 6

think apparatus with which we t.
EDUCATION, 2

If you...t. about your physical or moral condition
ILLNESS, 2

I never t. of the future
FUTURE, 3

people would sooner die than t.
THINKING, 3

time to t. before I speak
SPEECH, 4

You can't t. rationally on an empty stomach
THINKING, 2

thinkers not always the justest t.
THINKING, 1

thirst the t. to come
DRINKING, 11

thought What was once t.
IDEAS, 1

thoughts Keep off your t. from things that are past
PAST, 6

thousand What's a t. dollars
MONEY, 8

threat one can almost always see in a little girl the t. of a woman
CHILDREN, 6

three t. of us in this marriage
ADULTERY, 3

who sneaked into my room at t. o'clock this morning
COMPLAINTS, 1

throat A good listener is a good talker with a sore t.
SPEECH, 16

throne A tavern chair is the t.
DRINKING, 8

tide the full t. of human existence is at Charing-Cross
LONDON, 1

tiger man wants to murder a t. he calls it sport
HUNTING, 4

time Aging...the only...way to live a long t.
AGE, 1

I shall lose no t. in reading it
EXCUSES, 2

not had the t. to make it shorter
VERBOSITY, 1

the original good t. that was had by all
SEX, 5

T. is on our side
PROGRESS, 5

T....prevents everything from happening at once
TIME, 2

title Because of my t., I was the first
COURAGE, 1

title-page The book written against fame... has the author's name on the t.
HYPOCRISY, 2

tobacco who lives without t.
SMOKING, 4

today Its history dates from t.
ROYALTY, 2

together two people living t. for 25 years without having a cross word
WEDDINGS, 12

toil To t. and not to seek for rest
SELFLESSNESS, 1

tomorrow Drop...what t. may bring...count as profit every day that Fate allows you
PRESENT, 2

tongue One t. is sufficient for a woman
WOMEN, 10

woman's weapon is her t.
MEN AND WOMEN, 4

Tony T....he immatures with age
INSULTS, 7

toothache conquers all things except poverty and t. LOVE, 10
man with t....teeth are sound ENVY, 1
philosopher that could endure the t. ENDURANCE, 5
top I started at the t. and worked my way down ACHIEVEMENT, 7
There is always room at the t. AMBITION, 5
When you reach the t. SUCCESS, 3
torch Truth, like a t. TRUTH, 5
tour The time to enjoy a European t. TRAVEL, 1
trade No nation was ever ruined by t. BUSINESS, 4
same t....conversation ends in a conspiracy BUSINESS, 10
tragedy A single death is a t. STATISTICS, 3
travels A man t. the world over HOME, 3
treason T. doth never prosper BETRAYAL, 2
trouble a lot of t....most of which had never happened WORRY, 1
art of looking for t. OCCUPATIONS, 94
true Mr. Speaker, I said the honorable member was a liar it is t. and I am sorry for it APOLOGIES, 2
trust Never t. a husband too far WEDDINGS, 18
truth a t. universally acknowledged WEDDINGS, 2
Beauty is t., t. beauty BEAUTY, 2
before the t. has got its boots on LYING, 1
can only find t. with logic if you have already found t. LOGIC, 2
Every man has a right to utter what he thinks t. FREEDOM, 2
facts must never get in the way of t. OCCUPATIONS, 66
It takes two to speak the t. TRUTH, 7
Some men love t. so much TRUTH, 3
the t. shall make you free TRUTH, 2
t. is the uncharred rock SCIENCE, 2
T., like a torch TRUTH, 5
t. that makes men free TRUTH, 1
whatever remains, however improbable, must be the t. TRUTH, 4
writers regard t. as their most valuable possession OCCUPATIONS, 33
truths There are no new t. TRUTH, 6
try t. everything once EXPERIENCE, 1
tunnel light at the end of the t.... PESSIMISM, 2
turn I wouldn't have left a t. unstoned CRITICISM, 13
world would begin to t. the other way PROGRESS, 1
turning Life is a maze in which we take the wrong t. LIFE, 3
Tweedledee 'Contrariwise,' continued T. LOGIC, 1
twenty the first t. years YOUTH, 8
twenty-one confidence of t. YOUTH, 5
twice desire to be praised t. PRAISE, 3
Literature...something that will be read t. OCCUPATIONS, 60

two It takes t. to speak the truth TRUTH, 7
what can t. do against so many SPEECHES, 27

U

unanimity Our agenda is now exhausted....we find ourselves in such complete u. AGREEMENT, 3
underdogs never find an Englishman among the u. ENGLAND, 11
underemployed necessary to be slightly u. LEISURE, 2
understand child of five would u. this SIMPLICITY, 1
if he could make *me* u....it would be clear to all UNDERSTANDING, 2
too clever to u. PREJUDICE, 1
You suddenly u. something...in a new way EDUCATION, 8
understanding Most men...give evidence against their own u. SPEECH, 7
understood Only one man ever u. me UNDERSTANDING, 1
uneatable the unspeakable in full pursuit of the u. HUNTING, 7
uneducated Democracy...government by the u. DEMOCRACY, 2
unfaithful better to be u. ADULTERY, 5
universe specializing in the U. UNIVERSE, 1
take his attention away from the u. PRAYER, 1
the better ordering of the u. UNIVERSE, 2
unpack three weeks after you u. TRAVEL, 1
unpaid A promise made is a debt u. PROMISES, 2
unpopular society where it is safe to be u. FREEDOM, 7
unspeakable the u. in full pursuit of the uneatable HUNTING, 7
unstoned I wouldn't have left a turn u. CRITICISM, 13
unused left over from last year u. ADVICE, 2
up I saw it at a disadvantage – the curtain was u. CRITICISM, 13
use What is the u. of a new-born child TECHNOLOGY, 1
useless most beautiful things...are the most u. BEAUTY, 4

V

vain V. are the thousand creeds BELIEF, 2
valet difference between a man and his v. OCCUPATIONS, 109
value All knowledge is of itself of some v. KNOWLEDGE, 3
the price of everything and the v. of nothing CYNICISM, 2
values ideas are of more importance than v. INTELLECT, 2
Van Gogh V.'s ear for music INSULTS, 6
variety custom stale her infinite v. COMPLIMENTS, 3

vegetarianism V. is harmless enough
HEALTH AND HEALTHY LIVING, 1
venerability If you live long enough, the v.
factor creeps in
AGE, 24
verification bring about the v. of his own
prophecies
PROPHECY, 1
verse no v. can give pleasure…that is written
by drinkers of water
DRINKING, 6
vestry I will see you in the v. after service
OCCUPATIONS, 36
vice This v. brings in one hundred million
francs…every year
SMOKING, 5
V. is its own reward
VICE, 1
victims Man…on friendly terms with the v.…
he eats
HYPOCRISY, 1
Victoria If this is the way Queen V. treats her
prisoners
COMPLAINTS, 2
views Whenever you accept our v.
AGREEMENT, 2
vines advise his clients to plant v.
MISTAKES, 3
violence V. is the repartee of the illiterate
VIOLENCE, 1
virginity losing my v. as a career move
PURITY, 2
that v. could be a virtue
PURITY, 4
virtue name a v. that brings in as much
revenue
SMOKING, 5
the v. of pigs in a litter
SOCIETY, 2
to practise five things…perfect v.
VIRTUE, 1
Woman's v. is man's…invention
VIRTUE, 2
virtues No one gossips about…secret v.
GOSSIP, 1
voice The higher the v.
INTELLECT, 5
vow better…not v., than…v. and not pay
PROMISES, 1
vulgar Arguments…v. and often unconvincing
ARGUMENTS, 6

W

wages Home art gone and ta'en thy w.
LEAVING, 11
Wagstaff a disgrace to our family name of W.
FAMILY, 4
wait I can w.
PATIENCE, 2
who only stand and w.
SERVICE, 1
waiting w. for the cock to crow
BETRAYAL, 3
walk Golf is a good w. spoiled
SPORT, 11
walks She w. in beauty
COMPLIMENTS, 1
wallet a crowd like that…brings a lump to my
w.
MONEY, 16
want give the public what they w. to see and
they'll come out for it
FUNERALS, 6
war As long as w. is regarded as wicked WAR, 4
twenty seconds of w. to destroy
WAR, 1
When the rich wage w.
POVERTY, 5
water no verse can give pleasure…that is
written by drinkers of w.
DRINKING, 6
Streets full of w.
PLACES, 1
w. flowed like champagne
ABSTINENCE, 4
w. still keeps falling over
PLACES, 2
way woman has her w.
MEN AND WOMEN, 6
wayside If you see anybody fallen by the w.
CHARITY, 2

weak Idleness…the refuge of w. minds
IDLENESS, 1
wealth God shows his contempt for w.
MONEY, 11
W. is like sea-water
GREED, 2
weaned w. on a pickle
APPEARANCE, 6
weapon woman's w. is her tongue
MEN AND WOMEN, 4
weariness much study is a w. of the flesh
BOOKS, 1
wedding A man looks pretty small at a w.
WEDDINGS, 23
weed What is a w.
GOOD, 3
weep w. for her sins at the other
ADULTERY, 2
welcome Advice is seldom w.
ADVICE, 1
well as w. off as if he were rich
MONEY, 2
kingdom of the w. and the kingdom of the
sick
ILLNESS, 3
reward of a thing w. done
SUCCESS, 4
wheat An editor…separates the w. from the
chaff
OCCUPATIONS, 61
when w. a man should marry
WEDDINGS, 4
where W. were you fellows when the paper
was blank
OCCUPATIONS, 58
white I used to be Snow W.
PURITY, 5
When the w. man came we had the land
RELIGION, 6
White House gathered together at the W.
SPEECHES, 4
who w. you are, you aren't anybody
FAME, 4
widow you, my dear, will be my w.
JEALOUSY, 1
wife A loving w. will do anything
MARRIAGE, 8
A man should not insult his w. publicly
MARRIAGE, 14
remorse for what you have thought about
your w.
MARRIAGE, 11
single man…must be in want of a w.
WEDDINGS, 2
The husband frae the w. despises
WEDDINGS, 8
with a w. to tell him what to do WORK, 7
will His right was clear, his w. was strong
RIGHT, 1
Man has his w.
MEN AND WOMEN, 6
We have to believe in free w.
FREEDOM, 6
will-power There is no such thing as a great
talent without great w.
ACHIEVEMENT, 1
wind fills a man with w. and self-righteousness
HEALTH AND HEALTHY LIVING, 2
what w. is to fire
LEAVING, 4
words but w.
SPEECH, 2
wine days of w. and roses
MORTALITY, 1
use a little w. for thy stomach's sake
DRINKING, 4
w. was a farce and the food a tragedy
FOOD, 3
wisdom in much w. is much grief
WISDOM, 1
privilege of w. to listen
KNOWLEDGE, 2

Silence is…full of potential w.   SPEECH, 9

wise a w. father   FAMILY, 7

wiser Be w. than other people   WISDOM, 2

the old have rubbed it into the young that
they are w.   AGE, 13

wish most…w. they were the only one alive   CONCEIT, 1

wit Brevity is the soul of w.   SPEECHES, 21

I have neither w., nor words, nor worth   SPEECHES, 22

wither Age cannot w. her   COMPLIMENTS, 3

wives husbands and w….belong to different
sexes   MEN AND WOMEN, 1

The others were only my w.   JEALOUSY, 1

W. are young men's mistresses   WEDDINGS, 3

woman A diplomat…always remembers a w.'s
birthday   AGE, 11

A man is only as old as the w.   AGE, 12

Any w. who understands the problems of
running a home   OCCUPATIONS, 100

It's a sort of bloom on a w.   CHARM, 1

Once a w. has given you her heart   WOMEN, 12

one can…see in a little girl the threat of a w.   CHILDREN, 6

One tongue is sufficient for a w.   WOMEN, 10

Twenty years of romance makes a w. look
like a ruin   MARRIAGE, 15

When a w. behaves like a man   WOMEN, 7

w. has her way   MEN AND WOMEN, 6

w. seldom asks advice   WOMEN, 1

W. will be the last thing civilized by Man   WOMEN, 9

women Few w. care to be laughed at   RIDICULE, 1

Men don't understand anything about w.   MEN AND WOMEN, 2

proclaiming that w. are brighter than men   FEMINISM, 1

proper function of w.   WOMEN, 6

Why are w….so much more interesting to
men   MEN AND WOMEN, 11

w.…not so young as…painted   WOMEN, 3

w. require both   WOMEN, 4

W.'S RIGHTS NOW   FEMINISM, 3

word Good isn't the w.   CRITICISM, 3

Tears wash out a W.   DESTINY, 1

words neither wit, nor w., nor worth   SPEECHES, 22

W. are…the most powerful drug   SPEECH, 11

w. but wind   SPEECH, 2

w. once spoke…never be recall'd   SPEECH, 14

You can stroke people with w.   SPEECH, 5

work I like w.; it fascinates me   IDLENESS, 2

no w., nor device, nor knowledge…in the
grave   WORK, 2

only place where success comes before w.   SUCCESS, 5

W. is the curse of the drinking classes   WORK, 12

W. is the grand cure   WORK, 3

world A man travels the w. over   HOME, 3

good deed in a naughty w.   GOOD, 5

I…pass through this w. but once   MORTALITY, 6

joy that a man is born into the w.   CHILDREN, 2

the w., the flesh, and the devil   OCCUPATIONS, 71

worlds we live in the best of all possible w.   OPTIMISM, 1

worse Dublin, though…much w. than London   PLACES, 8

worth W. seeing? yes   IRELAND, 2

worthy give the teachers stipends w. of the
pains   OCCUPATIONS, 117

is not w. to live   SMOKING, 4

wounds To fight and not to heed the w.   SELFLESSNESS, 1

writer Asking a working w….about critics   OCCUPATIONS, 43

best way to become a successful w.   OCCUPATIONS, 27

protect the w.   BUREAUCRACY, 1

writers No regime has ever loved great w.   OCCUPATIONS, 32

w. regard truth as their most valuable
possession   OCCUPATIONS, 33

writes Moving Finger w.   DESTINY, 1

wrong A door is what a dog is…on the w. side
of   DOGS, 2

Of course not…I may be w.   UNCERTAINTY, 1

our country, right or w.   PATRIOTISM, 1

responsible and w.   RESPONSIBILITY, 2

support me when I am…w.   SUPPORT, 1

there is nothing w. with America   AMERICA, 2

Yes, once…I thought I had made a w.
decision   MISTAKES, 2

wrote blockhead ever w. except for money   OCCUPATIONS, 30

Y

yacht I had to sink my y. to make my guests
go home   PARTIES, 1

yet A young man not y.   WEDDINGS, 4

but not y.   MORALITY, 1

young aged diplomats…bored than for y. men
to die   DIPLOMACY, 1

All that the y. can do for the old   AGE, 21

Most women are not so y. as they are painted   WOMEN, 3

The atrocious crime of being a y. man   YOUTH, 6

the old have rubbed it into the y.   AGE, 13

The y. always have the same problem   YOUTH, 2

The y. have aspirations   AGE, 19

to make me y. again   SURVIVAL, 1

You can be y. without money   MONEY, 17

younger I'm y. than that now   YOUTH, 3

youngest not even the y. of us   IMPERFECTION, 3

youth Y. is something very new   YOUTH, 1

Y. will come…beat on my door   YOUTH, 4

NAME INDEX

Burke, Thomas PRAISE, 1
Burns, George AGE, 4
Burns, Robert FAILURE, 1; OCCUPATIONS, 41;
WEDDINGS, 8
Burton, Richard OCCUPATIONS, 2
Burton, Robert ENGLAND, 1
Bussy-Rabutin LEAVING, 4
Butler, Samuel DOGS, 1; HYPOCRISY, 1; ILLNESS, 1;
PRAISE, 2; PROGRESS, 2; SPEECH, 2; TRUTH, 3; WOMEN, 4
Byron, Henry James GAMES, 2
Byron, Lord COMPLIMENTS, 1; LEAVING, 5

C

Cabell, James OPTIMISM, 1; PESSIMISM, 1
Caine, Michael SUCCESS, 3
Callaghan, James LYING, 1
Cameron, James OCCUPATIONS, 66
Campbell, Thomas OCCUPATIONS, 34
Canetti, Elias ANIMALS, 2; DEATH, 4
Canning, George FRIENDSHIP, 2
Carey, Dr George RELIGION, 4
Carlyle, Jane Welsh INJUSTICE, 1
Carlyle, Thomas BELIEF, 3; BOOKS, 2; GREATNESS, 1;
OCCUPATIONS, 125; PUBLIC, 2; WORK, 3
Carr, Jesse POWER, 3
Carrel, Alexis INTELLECT, 3
Carrington, Lord SCIENCE, 1
Carroll, Lewis LOGIC, 1
Carter, Jimmy BUREAUCRACY, 2
Cartland, Barbara SNOBBERY, 1
Cary, Joyce ADULTERY, 2; ART, 2
Catherwood, Mary FRIENDSHIP, 3
Chamfort, Nicolas INGRATITUDE, 1; LAUGHTER, 1
Chamfort, Sébastien OCCUPATIONS, 48
Chandler, Raymond APPEARANCE, 1; DRINKING, 5
Chanel, Coco WOMEN, 5; YOUTH, 1
Chaplin, Charlie LIFE, 2
Chateaubriand, Vicomte de CYNICISM, 1;
ORIGINALITY, 2
Chekhov, Anton OCCUPATIONS, 3
Chesterfield, Earl of ADVICE, 1; IDLENESS, 1;
WISDOM, 2
Chesterton, G. K. SPEECHES, 2; CRIME, 1; DEMOCRACY,
2; EDUCATION, 3; GOOD, 2; LOGIC, 2; MADNESS, 1; OBESITY, 2;
OCCUPATIONS, 67; SERIOUSNESS, 1
Chevalier, Maurice AGE, 5; LOVE, 3
Christie, Agatha WEDDINGS, 9
Churchill, Charles SPEECHES, 11
Churchill, Winston SPEECHES, 12, 13; DIPLOMACY, 2;
OCCUPATIONS, 126; PLACES, 2, 3, 4, 5; PRIDE, 1;
PRONUNCIATION, 1; RESPONSIBILITY, 1; SMOKING, 2; SPORT,
1; WORRY, 1
Ciano, Count Galeazzo DEFEAT, 1
Ciardi, John OCCUPATIONS, 15
Cibber, Colley FASHION, 1
Clemenceau, Georges AGE, 6; AMERICA, 1
Clinton, Bill AMERICA, 2
Clough, Arthur Hugh GOD, 2
Cobb, Irvin S. SPEECHES, 14
Cocks, Barnett BUREAUCRACY, 3
Colby, Frank More HUMOUR, 2
Coleridge, Samuel Taylor SINCERITY, 1

Colette SEX, 4
Collins, Joan MEN, 1
Colton, Charles Caleb EDUCATION, 4;
SPEECH, 3
Comfort, Alex ABSTINENCE, 2
Compton-Burnett, Ivy LEADERSHIP, 1
Conan Doyle, Arthur TRUTH, 4
Confucius IMPERFECTION, 1; VIRTUE, 1
Congreve, William SECRECY, 1
Connolly, Billy WEDDINGS, 10
Connolly, Cyril CHILDREN, 3; LIFE, 3; OCCUPATIONS, 68;
TALENT, 2
Conrad, Joseph CONSCIENCE, 1
Conran, Shirley LAZINESS, 1
Constable, John OCCUPATIONS, 16
Cook, Peter THEATRE, 1; UNIVERSE, 1
Coren, Alan DEMOCRACY, 3
Corneille, Pierre DUTY, 1; GIFTS, 1; SORROW, 1
Cornforth, John SCIENCE, 2
Coward, Noël HUMOUR, 5; MUSIC, 5
Crabbe, George OCCUPATIONS, 62
Crisp, Quentin FAMILY, 1, 2; MORALITY, 3; PRAYER, 1;
VICE, 1; YOUTH, 2
Cromwell, Oliver PUBLIC, 3
Crosby, Bing FRIENDSHIP, 4
Curzon, Lord MISTAKES, 1

D

d'Alençon, Duchesse COURAGE, 1
Daley, Janet RUTHLESSNESS, 1
Dali, Salvador OCCUPATIONS, 17
Daniels, R. G. APPEARANCE, 2
Darrow, Clarence Seward CLOTHES, 1
Darwin, Erasmus SPEECH, 4
Davies, W. H. ABSTINENCE, 3; KINDNESS, 1
Davis, Bette MEN, 2; OBITUARIES, 1; SEX, 5
Davis Jnr, Sammy FAME, 2
Davy, Humphry ART, 5
Day, Clarence Shepard FUNERALS, 3
Dayan, Moshe AGREEMENT, 2
Decatur, Stephen PATRIOTISM, 1
Deffand, Marquise du BEGINNING, 1
Degas, Edgar INJUSTICE, 2
Delille, Jacques FAMILY, 3
Delors, Jacques IDEALISM, 1
Denning, Lord ENGLAND, 2
Depew, Chauncey LAZINESS, 2
De Sica, Vittorio MORALITY, 9
Devonshire, Duke of SPEECHES, 15
De Vries, Peter EDUCATION, 5; POPULARITY, 1
Diana, Princess of Wales ADULTERY, 3;
CHILDREN, 4
Dickens, Charles SPEECHES, 3; BUSINESS, 2; CHILDREN,
5; HUNTING, 1; OCCUPATIONS, 80, 108
Dietrich, Marlene PLACES, 6
Diller, Phyllis ARGUMENTS, 2
Dillingham, Charles Bancroft FUNERALS, 4
Disraeli, Benjamin AGE, 7; CONCEIT, 3; EXCUSES, 2;
FOOD, 1; OCCUPATIONS, 25, 26, 95; ROYALTY, 1;
SELF-MADE MEN, 1
Dix, Dorothy MEN AND WOMEN, 1
Dix, Dom Gregory OCCUPATIONS, 35